ISN'T THAT RICH?

ISN'T THAT RICH?

Life Among the 1 Percent

WITHDRAWN

RICHARD KIRSHENBAUM

OPEN ROAD

INTEGRATED MEDIA

NEW YORK

Portions of this book have appeared previously, in slightly
different form, in the *New York Observer*.

Cover design by Andy Ross

978-1-5040-0732-0

Published in 2015 by Open Road Integrated Media, Inc.
345 Hudson Street
New York, NY 10014
www.openroadmedia.com

F. Scott had Zelda and I have Dana . . .

To have a friend or lover is divine; to have a muse is eternal.

Thank you, my darling, for your unwavering love and support, and for urging me not to change one word, for anyone.

I owe the column and the book entirely to you.

CONTENTS

FOREWORD

===================

Richard Kirshenbaum dedicates *Isn't That Rich?* to his wife, "for urging me not to change one word, for anyone." With all due respect to the author, that isn't precisely true.

Shortly after he started the column on which this book is based, for a local community newspaper, the *New York Observer*—which used to be called "the pink paper" even though it was, more accurately, printed on orange-y paper—he asked me out to lunch. As best I could tell, he wanted to pick my brain about what he could and couldn't get away with when covering the behavior of our city's rich.

I had long been a reader of the pink paper, and generally enjoyed it, because it did exactly what I have always done as a journalist: it sought to tell the truth about powerful and influential people. I started doing that instinctually decades ago when, after a brief spell as something akin to a promotion writer, helping rock stars sell their albums and concert tickets by making them out to be more heroic than they really were, I began telling the truth about them, and—oops—made myself a bit of a pariah.

Not long after that, I changed careers (not entirely by choice, as you might imagine) and briefly became an advertising copywriter. That wasn't how I met Richard, even though he was in advertising too, but it gave me the background necessary to appreciate his skills once I did encounter him after another career switch, this time back to journalism. I started writing about fashion and the folks who then pretty much exclusively consumed it (shorthand: the 1 percent).

Richard had some fashion clients, which is how we met, and, I think, how we came to appreciate each other. He approached advertising the same way I approached fashion journalism, with tongue firmly in cheek and the rule book balancing on the lip of the trash.

Back then, I worked for one of the legends of journalism, an editor named Clay Felker. He'd founded the first magazine I adored, *New York*, which was one of the crucibles of what was called New Journalism, and was all about "tell the truth, damn the consequences, and do it in a way that's as entertaining as it is informative." I went to work for Felker when he started another publication, long since mostly forgotten, that was the spiritual forefather of the formerly pink paper Richard now writes for. I bring this up because at one of our first editorial meetings, Felker said something to the new staff that I have never forgotten concerning the 1 percenters who would be our main subjects: remember that you are *in* their world, but you are not *of* it, and you will succeed in covering them.

Which brings us back to the subject at hand, Richard's fine, funny, and informative book, which also has the virtue of being very entertaining, even if it doesn't exactly adhere to Clay Felker's dictum. Because, you see, at some point, Richard sold the advertising agency he founded and made a boatload of money, and now he lives on Fifth Avenue and eats at dives like Harry Cipriani, where a salad costs something like forty dollars. In other words, he is not only *in* the world he writes about in the pages that follow, he is *of* it, as well.

So it's a bit of a white lie to say that Richard hasn't changed one word for anyone. Well, not a white lie, precisely, but a misdirection. The kind of thing advertising folk do naturally. Because what I discovered after our lunch was that Richard does something I don't do. Or rather, Richard doesn't do something that I *do* do, which has sometimes gotten me into, well, deep doo-doo. I write about the 1 percent and name names and figure that if I tell maybe 80 percent of what I've been able to learn about them, which may be 70 percent of the truth about them, I've done a job I can be proud of.

Richard, on the other hand, tells, I'd estimate, 95 percent of what he's been able to learn about the 1 percent who are his friends and neighbors, and while he too may only get to that golden 70-percent-of-the-truth threshold, he seems not to get into the kind of trouble that made me somewhat radioactive among the more humorless denizens of Mr. Kirshenbaum's neighborhood. You know, the ones who think their doo-doo comes direct from Guerlain. Fortunately, a lot of Richard's friends, or at least those quoted herein, do have a sense of humor about themselves and their cohort, and you, lucky reader, get to dine on their dish.

Richard's secret is a simple one. He *doesn't* name names like I have always done. His approach is almost genial, even if the net effect is still outrageous. Which is probably why he lives on Fifth Avenue and has more money in the bank than I do. We still get together and talk shop and laugh, and somehow (especially since he usually pays for dinner) I don't hold his wealth against him. Or the fact that he's now invaded my turf. And, come to think of it, been rather quickly successful at it.

Maybe I should hate him. I just can't. He has a keen sense of perspective that some of his subjects lack. As he notes, he still flies commercial. I like that. I like his book, too. And I can pretty much guarantee that you will as well. But if you don't, don't call me for a refund. He's the one in and of the world of those who can afford to pay for guaranteed satisfaction.

Michael Gross

Michael Gross is the author of books including House of Outrageous Fortune, 740 Park, Rogues' Gallery, *and* Unreal Estate. *His writing has appeared in the* New York Times, New York, Vanity Fair, Esquire, GQ, *and countless other publications.*

ISN'T THAT RICH?

I.

EMBARRASSMENT OF RICHES

1. BILLIONAIRE BUZZKILL

They're Ruining the Fun for Mere Millionaires

AT THE TAIL END of the summer, I found myself in Millbrook, New York, the guest of a dashing blond sportsman who consistently beats me at squash. As we exited his stately Georgian mansion, I asked him if he preferred the tranquility of the country or whether he missed the electricity of Manhattan.

"Perhaps I would, if I were still relevant." He shrugged, tossing his squash gear into his vintage woodie station wagon.

"Relevant? You can't be serious," I said.

"I am. Honestly," he countered. "I'm 1990s money—in a new age—with one less zero." He sighed as we drove down the leafy lane to his club for a game of squash and a flight of dry martinis.

Over the past few years, New York has turned into a receiving line for billionaires. While the superrich and their attending lifestyles have dwarfed the average American success story, they have also depositioned the wealthy, creating a vast and palpable divide, not only between the haves and the have-nots, but the haves and have-mores.

While there may be fewer of them in New York City than one may imagine (under one hundred), billionaires' influence has spawned an era of excess, entitlement, grandiosity, and outright glitz not seen since the Roaring Twenties, causing their lesser-endowed peers to suffer from what I call *billionaire buzzkill.*

"*A millionaire* used to mean you've made it." A Master of the Universe decanted a beautiful bottle of Saint-Émilion. His staff hovered, bringing oversize crystal goblets and chic pressed linen napkins that were as thin as crepes and starched as a wimple. "Everyone wants to be Gatsby, without the car crash."

"Are you sure you want to drink in the living room?" I asked as he poured the ruby-red liquid above his white furniture.

"No worries," he said, taking a call from one of his many brokers, his pressed French cuffs slicing the air.

"So what's considered real money today, if you only happen to be a millionaire?"

"I would say a hundy."

"A hundy?"

"A hundred million. But not including your real estate. I mean investible assets."

"So a hundred gets you in the game?"

"Well, maybe two hundred," he said thoughtfully, swirling the red liquid dangerously over creamy white cashmere throws.

The .01 percent have had an enormous impact on the psyches of people formerly running New York and have taken the fun out of *la vida loca.* The resulting syndrome—let's call it millionaire malaise—includes symptoms such as loss of identity, the throwing in of the competitive towel, and Xanax- and chardonnay-level anxiety.

The terrace of Orsay seemed a perfect place to broach the subject of billionaire buzzkill with a standard-issue millionaire. Had he ever experienced it?

"Of course. Just when you think you've made it with your mackdaddy ten-million-dollar apartment, your wife comes home and says, 'So-and-so just bought a thirty-five-million-dollar apartment,' and you feel like a loser," he said.

"Does this happen a lot?"

"It happens at least once a week," he admitted. "You think you're a player, flying your family first class, then so-and-so asks for your tail number, and they look at you like you're taking the bus because you're flying commercial."

"Wow, that's a trip."

"You're excited for your recent art acquisition, and then they invite you to the opening of their new museum. Buzzkill. You spend your bonus buying your wife an eight-carat cushion-cut diamond, and her best friend calls it cute when she flashes the twenty. You're psyched you splurged for floor seats, and they're buying the team. Buzzkill. I need another glass of wine," he said, grimacing.

"Or I can throw you a charity dinner," I offered.

I paid a visit to an old friend whose family name adorns one of the city's most prominent cultural institutions. I wondered whether he had similar experiences, given his burnished stature. We sat in his cavernous Fifth Avenue apartment with family portraits looming.

"Understatement went out the window with Lehman," he said, sipping a Blackwell rum on the rocks. "Personally, I like walking around in my old khakis and a sweater with holes in the elbows. I like my hoboish style. Of course, you get no service."

"I'm not sure that's entirely the case," I countered.

"Look, I'm so far from being important now. I feel like a shrinking star with a bit of Yankee thrift. I'm just hunkering down. A person of modest wealth and achievement protecting the franchise," he said among the Corgis and chinoiserie.

"Well, take this apartment," I said. "Very few people could ever pass the board interview, no matter how much money they had."

"That's the point," he said. "Those people don't want to live here. They don't want to live by anyone else's rules."

The exclusivity of some of New York's toughest co-op boards has had a reverse effect. I recalled reading a recent article in the *Wall Street Journal* about one of New York's most prestigious co-ops hiring a public relations firm to help promote sales.

"In a way, it's good, because the new condos represent another product for another group," he observed. "People want to live in a co-op because they appreciate communal living with like-minded people living quietly, privately in understated elegance, not to mention the prewar details."

He continued: "There are quiet billionaires who live here, but you'd never know it. It's just that if you don't like being told 'no' and your wife has a personal publicist, it's probably better if you live on the West Side or Downtown."

"It's not my Madison Avenue anymore," Chic Brunette Heiress explained over sea breezes in her classic East Hampton sunroom, the low-key wicker set prompting me to recall the well-known quote about how it takes a few generations to actually understand wicker.

"Growing up in the city, I remember it as a small village, where I used to know everyone and . . . don't take this the wrong way, that I was somebody."

"And now?

"I walk up and down the avenue, I don't know many people, and they don't know me. Honestly, I don't even recognize the brands. A cashmere sweater costs as much as a small car. And who are all these people anyway? Hardly anyone speaks English." She sniffed.

"What is the biggest change since your days at [an elite private girls school]?"

"The tone has changed. The taste and the manners especially."

"Meaning?"

"The old-school wealthy do things a certain way. Handwritten notes instead of e-mail. Having dinner conversation without the person across from you on their cell phone the whole time. Texting has ruined a whole generation. Then there are what we call the new West Side billionaires. You know, the ones who live in those condos."

"And would you ever live there?"

"I wouldn't call that area living. More likely visiting."

"Well, it's all near the park, isn't it?"

"That's like saying there's no difference between East and West Hampton, even though they all share the same coastline. Can I get you a refill?" She surveyed the tinkling ice cubes in her glass.

I put in a call to a real estate agent who is known for prying loose all of those newly acquired hundies.

"Today, the superrich want to live in glass boxes," the *über*broker said, offering me a walking tour of the West Side as she navigated three digital devices and tottered on skyscraper heels.

"They want light, air. They want modern, contemporary. They want ceiling-height, recessed lighting. They want wall space for the art. They want glass, views, service. They want to do what they want when they want. They want to renovate, decorate. The whole shebang."

"They want a lot."

"And they get it."

"So, do you only sell condos?"

"I don't sell, I specialize," she said, applying dizzying red lipstick. "They sell themselves, even before they're built."

"What about co-ops?"

"Most of my clients don't have the time or patience to sit in a room with a bunch of fuddy-duddies judging them," she said, marching down CPW like General Patton in Louboutins.

"Do your clients even look at co-ops?"

"Mostly no. Some don't want to reveal all their financial info to a board," she added. "But most want a level of freedom and have zero tolerance for a restricted building. They don't want co-op rules like no dogs allowed and grandma taste. New York real estate is a gold mine, and there's hardly any great inventory. That said, condos have clearly outpriced co-ops in terms of price and changed the way the superrich look at the luxury market. In my opinion, it's where the supersmart money is going. Listen, I have to run." She looked at her diamond-encrusted, saucer-size timepiece.

"Where to?"

"I have an appointment to show a thirty-million-dollar apartment to, like, a twenty-year-old."

"Tech?"

"How did you know?" she asked, taking the bottle of water from her driver.

"A wild guess. So no co-op for him?"

"I'd like to see their faces when he shows up to that board interview in a hoodie," she said with a smirk. "Although he could buy and sell the lot of them."

———

"I really don't think it's only a new-money versus old-money thing," a billionaire philanthropist and political donor told me as we walked around the reservoir with the buildings on Fifth Avenue, CPW, and CPS providing an ironic tableaux.

"There are newly minted billionaires who value old-money pedigree and old-school billionaires who'd rather live in a Tribeca loft. That said, this happens every hundred years when new wealth is created and shakes up the old guard. And then both sides take potshots at each other," he said, sipping his Juice Press Fountain of Youth.

"How so?" I asked, drinking a Runa Energy.

"The old money says the new money is gauche and parvenu. And the new money has contempt for the establishment's moribund practices and strictures."

"Such as?"

"Let's say a restricted private club that allows one spouse to join and not the other. What's elegant about that?"

"Do you think billionaires are behaving badly?"

"Some behave poorly, and some, like our mayor, are quite hardworking and understated given his level of wealth. Then again, there's a certain mean-spiritedness to how old money views the new wealth."

"Such as?"

"The restrictive nature of certain clubs, co-ops, institutions are meant to keep certain people out. Now, there are equally prestigious options, and they're no longer the only game in town, which is about time. The co-op owners also get crazy knowing the new buildings are trading at huge premiums. It's actually great payback, literally. That's why I live in a townhouse. I have no patience for all this nonsense."

"Do you think it's particular to New York?"

"The international billionaires are coming here, because it's the safest and best place to be—an expensive insurance policy. What's playing out in New York is playing out on a national level. You have one mayoral candidate describing New York as a 'tale of two cities' and the mayor welcoming fellow billionaires to New York because they're good for the economy and tax burden. They both have a point."

"So you don't feel badly about all your hundies and billions?" I joked.

"I've worked hard for it all. Either we're capitalists or socialists! That's the problem today—the conflict, the indecision. . . . You can't have it both ways."

"Well, as long as you're happy," I said.

"It all goes back to what I think Plato said."

"What's that?"

"In order to be truly happy, you have to surround yourself with people less successful than yourself," he said, walking down the steps to a waiting town car.

"So do you practice what you preach?"

"Of course. Why do you think I'm spending time with you?" he joked in a nonjoking fashion, then slid in the backseat before the car sped away.

As I walked out of the park down Fifth Avenue, I marveled at the facade of the Metropolitan, as I always do, and thought there's nothing better than living in New York. But it just may be time to add a few new friends to the list.

2. THE CHANGING OF THE GUARD

The Old Guard Courts the New Guard
Because Cash Is King

IT MIGHT BE IRONIC that I happen to be sitting in Madrid in what is widely regarded as the world's *oldest* restaurant (drinking Rosado and sampling phallic white asparagus) writing about the *new guard* . . .

Botín (est. 1725), which Hemingway proclaimed in *The Sun Also Rises* as one of the best restaurants in the world, is all about the old and authentic, a warren of beamed ceilings and leaded glass. In Europe, the older institutions usually occupy the best locations. I view it as embracing the old and discovered, versus the new world—which celebrates the new, trendy, and undiscovered.

Two days before I had boarded the luxurious Iberia flight at Kennedy, I attended a house party on the East End. Best Man and his wife, whom we are so close with I have anointed her "Second Wife," were hosting an eclectic crowd at their architecturally significant home. The weekend proved to be a social workout, cramming as many as *eight* Fourth of July parties into just two days. As I was getting "my morning hangover coffee" at the Sagg Store, I ran into the scion of one of the bloodiest of blue-blooded families, which now seem to be ever increasingly in the minority.

"Happy Fourth, Richard," he said, his jaw so locked I wondered how words actually emanated. "How is your weekend?"

I revealed my social hangover and described the seaside party I'd attended at the home of one of New York's last great bachelors, where the party and favors never seem to end.

"Oh, you must take me one day," he pleaded. "I'd love to get on his list."

"List?" I said somewhat shocked. "I never took you for a social animal, James (not his real name)." In fact, I hardly ever thought he emerged from the grounds of his rambling but now seedy family compound and his fortresslike golf club that still somehow manages to exclude.

"I need to start hanging out with people who have *real* money," he opined.

"Real money as opposed to fake?" I asked.

"Look, you know the deal. Most of my friends are living on *fumes*," he said wearily. "It's less fun than it used to be."

After the lingering financial crisis, a sliver of rich have gotten richer, but a global cash crunch has emerged, not entirely causing a depression but, shall we say, an *international malaise*. The formerly well-to-do are making adjustments in order to preserve their once exuberant lifestyle. Some, in search of ready cash for businesses, charities, clubs, private schools, or their own social endeavors, have had to make allowances and become, shall we say, more *flexible*. Faced with conundrums and hard choices, old money now courts new money, and cash is King. And Queen.

Back from a beach walk, I happened upon four long, tanned legs interlocked like puzzle pieces on a chaise. International Playboy Posse (IPP) was in town from London with his twenty-one-year-old Russian model/actress girlfriend. Once settled in and dressed for dinner, we all convened on the terrace. IPP (who you get if you put Mick Jagger, Peter O'Toole, and a billionaire in a blender) and I shared a glass of rosé and immediately agreed on my theory that the new money, which was once shunned and mocked, is now being actively courted by old money.

"In London society, the aristocracy is being replaced by a fast European crowd that is defined by its fabulousness." He said this with a feline elegance you don't usually see in a man's man delivery.

"How does that work?" I asked, refilling his glass with some Domaine Ott to "lubricate" the conversation and hopefully pry any further valuable gems loose.

He shrugged. "Someone rich comes to town, makes a splash, and if they're known as having real money, there's interest and instant entrée. The old families are now reliant on these new people for shoots on their estates and such. Money can now buy you a ticket into a place like London. It wasn't always the case."

"Well, if it's bad in London, you should see what passes for good breeding in New York," I said with a laugh. I read a quote from an article about a new hot spot where someone actually said they liked it because it was " pretentious."

"Yes, you have these *garish* reality shows here and such. It's all so *tawdry* really. Then again, everyone likes a good female catfight, don't they, even in London."

"Does it go beyond London?"

"Absolutely," he declared in his punctuated accent. "We keep a boat in the South of France and it's down there for the Monaco Grand Prix, which is really the start of the social season since it's in May."

"That sounds fairly marvelous," I said, now understanding the length of his so-called boat.

"Yes. Then again, you see crowds of *awful* people arriving because they think that the glamorous world of Monaco will some-how rub off on them."

"Do people cater to you because you have big toys?"

"Yes." He laughed amiably. "Everyone likes the royal treatment, even the royals." He extended a long tailored arm to his model/actress girlfriend—"*Shall* we?"—indicating that he was ready to go to the next party and that we should all follow his playboy lead, which I was inclined to do.

"The biggest issue today is cash flow," a Californian businessman in Madrid declared over the extensive and sumptuous buffet breakfast at the Villa Magna. Although it is hot and sticky in July in Spain, the businessmen were all turned out in navy serge suits.

"It's one of the reasons I sold my business to the private equity fund." He had the Madrileños nodding at hello. "I needed the backup."

"We all need cash," they agreed. "It's a global issue."

Since I was traveling alone, I had been seated directly in ear-shot of a business meeting over steaming espresso. With his boom-ing American voice and Texan business partner, the man speaking seemed to be wooing the old guard with tales of available cash and credit. Clearly, with Spain's notorious unemployment and economy, the Americans with checkbooks were in town.

"You must come to my club," an elegant Madrileño offered in his heavy accent, swooning at the word *cash*. "You must come. It is ze best private club in Madrid."

"My son is doing an exchange program in September," the Cali-fornian said.

"He must come and see me," the Spanish grandee said. "We will take very good care of him."

"Does your company ever do internships?" he inquired bluntly. "I mean if we do business together?"

"More coffee?" the waitress asked me suddenly, interrupting my eavesdropping reverie.

I remembered a recent conversation in New York. "Sometimes I wonder if it's a cliché that the newly rich have such bad manners, but generalities are a bit unfair," Our Lady of the East River declared over anemic petite hors d'oeuvres at one of the few Manhattan pri-vate clubs that still discourages press mentions. We both picked up a slightly limp puff pastry filled with some overly mayonnaised concoction. "Truly, one has to wear earplugs, they have such loud voices," she said, delivering the searing indictment.

I really couldn't fault Our Lady, who regularly declares that anyone over a certain age should be able to say what they want—and she clearly does. Our Lady (my friend's great-aunt), who does a great deal of fund-raising for a select group of worthy charities, often has to interact with the new money types for her philanthropic efforts. "As we all know," Our Lady illuminated the conversation, "a coveted slot as a cochair or a sizable donation ensures the couple's name appearing on the host committee engraved invitation. Hosting an event also guarantees table sales for the events and is a draw for people who like seeing their names in full view with more established names." Her clear blue eyes and forthright manner made it hard to argue with her point of view. (Why is it that woman of this stock all start to look like George Washington at a certain age?)

"Now it would also be unfair to say that all my *new friends* act this way," she offered. "There are some who are elegant and donate anonymously. Most are very generous. I actually like a few of them but I really draw the line at *dinner*." She lamented, "They shout so much and, well, the way they talk to the waitstaff! It's really too much for me." She leaned in. "So my trick is that if I have to go with a big donor, I go to *loud* restaurants"—she mentioned a few—"so as not to be embarrassed."

After so many summers in Italy where the new money tourists consistently raise the decibel level and eyebrows of fellow European diners, it was hard not to see her point. Many American travelers do have a tendency to shout and dominate low-ceilinged restaurants, and I can attest to not wanting to be associated with the shrill, not to mention their unattended, undisciplined, and ill-behaved progeny.

"That said, you do take in quite a substantial amount of money for your charities from your new friends," I had to counter.

"My dear, the new people are the only ones who actually donate. My group is lucky to dust off the old tux. Most of these people are first-generation success stories and they do want to give back. It's very admirable. I have great respect and like many of them a great deal."

"So you would have them over?"

"Of course, dear. They're *all* welcome to [her East River Place abode]. Honestly, I'd rather have them at the apartment; I just can't abide a tête-à-tête at [two discreet old-school restaurants where you can hear the napkin drop].

"I even like some of those wives of theirs. They all have such perfect teeth. Although they tend to *drench* themselves in parfum . . . there's such a thing as *moderation*," she implored. "It's just I can't have people virtually shouting when I am eating. It's not good for the digestion. And the gargantuan *portions* they order. Why, it's obscene. And if I hear one more person say 'you don't know who I am' when they get the wrong table, I am ready to return the check."

And, with that, Our Lady closed the conversation.

"They should be lucky to have me," Handsome Harry declared at the plush bar of the Majestic Hotel in Barcelona. I had run into HH, or as some people refer to him, *Cash and Charry.* As we caught up over drinks and salted snacks, Cash and Charry revealed he had just gained admittance to one of the most prestigious golf clubs back home in the US of A and notably one of the hardest membership lists to crack. The fact that he was not only well turned out, a scratch golfer, and had sold his tech business for *mucho dinero* didn't hurt his chances.

"Not that I'm *not* excited, but many of the members couldn't afford to join the clubs they belong to or the co-ops they live in. Regardless of what they say, membership to some of the clubs is dwindling and not everyone can afford the minimum or the assessments, so they need some new blood." He shrugged. "You know, people like me to pay the bills. I know the score," he admitted, running his fingers through his thick, glossy hair.

"They're all awful snobs, and every five minutes they remind me that their fathers or grandfathers were members. Then I know they'll tap me when it comes time for the new roof."

"Well, that's a very honest appraisal, Harry," I said, clinking glasses of sherry *blanco.*

"I mean, the food and facilities are better at your club, but"— he shrugged again—"everyone wants to belong to somewhere their friends couldn't get in. It's great for business. Everyone wants to get invited to [legendary club]. You must come."

"I've played there before. It's really wonderful, although the food is fairly inedible. They do have a very well-stocked wine cellar, though," I happily admitted.

"Well, you know that's what's important: the liquor."

"So where are you off to after Barcelona?" I inquired.

"Well, Jasmine (HH's model girlfriend) and I are meeting the boat we rented and then we go to Saint-Tropez and then down to Monaco. Jasmine has never been before. I love Saint-Tropez, but she insisted she wants to go to Monte Carlo. You know, this is her first trip to Europe and she wants to go to all the best places."

"Smart girl."

"And of course, I had to buy her a whole set of luggage before she came. We can't go to Monaco with old luggage."

"Louis Vuitton?"

"How did you know? It's the best."

"And when do you go back to the States?"

"Well, we'll be back before Labor Day. I'm throwing a fundraiser at my Hamptons house for some charity. You and your wife should come."

"What charity?" I asked.

"I'll have to ask Jasmine. It's her gig. She wanted to be cochair, and she gets to wear a long dress and gets her name on the invitation. You know how women are. She wants to do good and get her photo in [x magazine]."

"She sounds determined."

"Once the society girls get to know her, they'll love her. Although some are jealous because she looks so HOT in Chanel."

"Yes," I said, thinking of Jasmine having dinner with Our Lady and what that conversation would be like. . . . "Well, so glad to see you, Harry. I'm glad to hear things are going so well for you. Enjoy Monte Carlo."

"You know what I always say, Richard. *With money you get honey.*"

After Spain, Capri sparkled and beckoned like a contessa's antique cabochon emerald, the kind I sometimes see nestled into a dowager's fading bosom along the Via Camerelle.

It's not untrue that I prefer risotto to paella, so being back on Tiberius's isle always makes my summer. Capri, though, as a summer playground attracts variety, and within minutes of arriving and walking through the piazza I ran into no fewer than five couples in various states of bathing and shopping attire. The boating crowd varies a bit from the hotel crowd, and I observed a few odd pairings and groups (the poor and the titled and the rich and the vulgar). I mentioned this to a friend in the boating circle when I observed a couple whose yacht was the size of a cruise ship and stocked with a vast array of guests, some it seemed they hardly knew.

"That's because they have a few *professional guests* on board for entertainment," he said, window-shopping at the Tod's store for driving shoes.

"What do you mean by professional?"

"Oh, come now, Richard. You know the score. So-and-so provides the Big Boat and then they invite an assorted group of 'names' who are happy to freeload and provide entertainment and give the group a bit of polish. Why in the world would Gunther and Cosima Von Snap (not their real identities) mix with that horrid group. All the truly elegant people are on sailboats anyway." He turned up his nose.

"Why do they go?" I said, still not fully understanding.

"They get a free vacation. They're *fed, bed, and flown* because they have the name, but they don't have a POT. It's the story as old as time."

"Whose story?" I asked naively.

"Listen, some of these old trust-fund babies live like pensioners. Then they meet the gravy train and once again, it's flying private and big boats and trips to St. Barths. They're back in the high life on someone else's dime."

"Isn't that a great deal of *work*?"

"Not if the only place you can go for the summer is a public beach."

"And do they get spending money too?" I marveled.

"Listen, I will not say *who,* but I actually saw one husband reaching into his pocket, pulling out a roll of bills big enough to choke a horse, and peeling off fifties to give to not one but two or three wives . . . as if the women were all on the payroll."

"And what does he get in return?" I asked.

"The pleasure of their company," he said as he walked into the shoe store. "Like that article you wrote on paid friends."

If you really want to know what's going on in Capri, all you need to do is ask the strolling photographers who make their living taking photos of passing tourists.

It's a respected profession in Capri and harkens back to the days when American stars arrived as they snapped away, long before iPhones and selfies.

"How is your season?" I asked my old pal Fabrizio, who is one of the island's premier paparazzi and always gives me the update on which nationality is in residence and who has the money. Each year varies; some years the Americans are omnipresent, then the Japanese, then the Russians, whoever it seems has the money that year.

"*Bene,*" he said. "This year is good. The hotels are full."

"Who is here this year?" I asked as I usually do.

"This year we have plenty of Brazilians. They make all the big parties."

"Americans?"

"Yes, of course. But not as much as last year. This year it's the Brazilians and the Australians. They make ALL the parties."

We posed for shots as we waited for the Silver Fox, who had coptered in from Rome the night before with his paramour, L'actrice. We lingered on the terrace of the island's enduring and fabulous social hub, the Grand Hotel Quisisana, before heading down to the beach club.

"No one cares about them anymore," said L'actrice as she adjusted her chic straw hat and movie star glasses on the scenic terrace of La Fontelina. "Fashion people, entertainment people. That's where you want to be. Hire a PR person and you're the new guard."

"In what way?" I asked, twirling the homemade *linguine aglio olio* and looking out at the iconic Faraglioni.

"People believe what they're told."

"Which is?"

"Who is relevant, interesting. Important."

L'actrice then referenced her brief, first marriage to the son of one of Hollywood's greatest and most famous American musical stars from the 1940s.

"When I was married to Bradley (not his real name) I spent *a lot* of time with the old guard; they just revered his father, who was *very* conservative. Besides all wanting to sleep with me, I found them all very dry. No joie de vivre. Plus they all fly *coach*. No one in that crowd flies private." She sniffed. "They're just boring with a sense of entitlement."

"How long were you married?" I asked, pouring her a liberal glass of Scolca Gavi di Gavi.

"Two years. I was so young. He was wonderful, but when there was a crisis he was always out duck hunting. It just wasn't meant to be."

"And now?"

"Now, I just hired a great PR agent from [notable, Hollywood PR firm] and it's my time. I did the old-money thing in my first marriage, now I spend time with the new guard. It's the changing of the guard, you know, and the old guard needs the new guard. No one cares about the old families anymore. They are done!" she declared. "One of the benefits of having money is being with interesting people, movers and shakers," she went on, twirling her ring, at least ten carats of sapphires and diamonds. L'actrice, who also comes from one of the wealthiest and prominent families, can do what she wants and has no intention of becoming passé.

"So you really have no desire to be in that world anymore?"

"None."

"But do you find the new guard courting you now?"

"Of course. And I hate to think that people just want to spend the weekend (at their seaside mansion) in the Hamptons or catch a ride on the plane," she said. "But I do it. And some are very lovely." She paused. "I like being with the exciting people now."

She downed her glass. "When I'm dead, I'll sleep."

Each time I see the impressive ruins that Tiberius constructed on Capri, as I make the strenuous hike up to the Villa Jovis, I marvel at the level of ancient Roman construction, from seaside palaces to bathing systems that clearly cost a fortune and must have had lingering effects on Roman society. Besides living out his days in luxury and rumored debauchery, Tiberius was also known for throwing his wives off the soaring cliff when he tired of them. When he died, he did leave an impressive old-money fortune to his heir. Unfortunately, his choice of an heir was Caligula, who went right through Tiberius's fortune of 2,700,000,000 sesterces, which according to historians eventually led to the decline of the Julio Claudian dynasty.

Well, I thought, as I hiked my way up to the impressive and soaring Arco Naturale, *it does seem the quest for cash and the high life is eternal.*

3. RISE OF THE ART INSTA-COLLECTORS

Buying Big Names They Don't Even Love

A NUMBER OF YEARS BACK, I attended a dinner in one of New York City's legendary apartment buildings, hosted by a now-divorced art-collecting couple. I was seated between a mogul's wife and an actress known for her lewd mouth, wearing couture but desperately in need of a bath. The conversation turned to art collecting, one of the Upper East Side's most popular topics after real estate and renovations.

"So are you a collect-uh?" Madame Mogul turned to me, looking over my shoulder as we chatted.

As the cater waiter served grilled salmon, she listed her current acquisitions and art fair events she and her husband had attended in recent months. Clearly, the couple had a voracious appetite, but not for salmon.

"And what do you collect?" she asked in the dutiful fashion of someone primarily interested in herself.

I politely revealed a few midcentury Modern names.

She looked at me wide-eyed, aghast that I hadn't listed the trendy, contemporary superstars her peers collect. "Oh, so you collect dead people?" she asked.

"I hadn't looked at it that way," I said.

"Does anyone here collect syringes?" The actress laughed sardonically.

I was brought up to view art as inspiration, not a commodity to be traded like natural gas. When I was in my early thirties and able to afford my first real piece, I consulted a close friend's father, a legendary collector whose name graces a wing at the Metropolitan. I asked for his opinion on an impressionist drawing at one of the auction houses. Later that week, I received his verdict.

"It's not so much a fully realized drawing as it is a glorified signature. Better to wait for a good picture that you love," he said in his lilting European accent. "A painting or drawing is like a woman. You must love her in the evening and also must love her when you wake up in the morning."

Things have drastically changed since that conversation, owing to the rise of insta-collectors: art consumers motivated less by passion and more by ego, money, and social access.

"A dealer I know quite well who caters to this crowd used to call it big swinging dick art," a reed-thin consultant told me over a salmon roll at Morimoto. She lamented that an art collection is viewed much the same as a stock portfolio.

"I've had clients who have no idea who the artist is they're actually bidding on," she said. "One couple who spent millions on a piece—I actually had to correct their pronunciation of the artist's name. It's like they bought a Givenchy and pronounced it Give-IN-chy and not Jzhiv-on-shee." The consultant shrugged. "But I made a good commission on that one, and the piece has already tripled in value."

At a top auction house like Christie's or Sotheby's, evening sales have the frisson of a courtside Knicks game, along with the seating hierarchy.

When I started to collect and immerse myself in the art world, a friend of mine, a well-known real estate magnate, kindly offered me his tickets for an evening sale he couldn't attend.

I remember the sensation of arriving a bit late and being directed to my friend's floor seats. "I know he collects, but I didn't realize he's at this level," I heard a woman in Chanel exclaim as I navigated my way to the assigned seat. I was wedged between a poster child for plastic surgery and what appeared to be a South American bon vivant, given the French cuffs and frothy pochette.

It was both exciting and unnerving as the major lots were revealed. After a frenzied bidding war, the hushed crowds burst into applause. That people actually clap for the person willing to spend the most money was just one sign that art collecting has turned into a blood sport.

That's partly because of the herd mentality surrounding it. Like fashion or décor, choosing art should be a matter of taste. But collections are so often dictated by one of an army of architects, art consultants, and decorators who have stepped up to help undereducated overspenders buy the same art everyone else has.

"People choose decorators the way the wife chooses a handbag. 'You have so-and-so; I need to use them too,'" a seasoned collector said, shrugging over an espresso and a smoked salmon tartine at Via Quadronno. "Now all these people hire art consultants who procure the art. By the time the project is finished, there is very little individual taste. It's like the way you see all these girls with flat-ironed hair, a hobo bag, jeans, and high heels."

Dana and I were having Sunday brunch at the Park Avenue apartment of an art advisor who has hosted and advised some of Wall Street's and Hollywood's biggest names over the years. Our hostess pointed to the artfully set buffet. "Tuna? Salmon salad?"

As we ate, she recalled growing up on Fifth Avenue, when collecting art was less of a game. "They were a staid, older, intellectual group," she said. "There were also few young collectors."

She sipped her Earl Grey as she turned toward the seven-figure portrait presiding over her dining room mantel. "I've seen it go from couture to department store."

A friend's regal mother concurred. "Of course, the old-school collectors find the whole thing absurd," she confided over high tea at one of Manhattan's most discreet private clubs, housed in a belle époque mansion. Her blond lacquered hair, set in a genteel coif, recalled when women went to beauty parlors and not salons.

"I remember going to school in Paris as a young girl and spending weeks at the Louvre. It was divine. When my husband and I were first married, we went to an old-line gallery and purchased our first *nature morte*. While it was less expensive then compared to today, we still put it on a layaway plan. It took us a year to pay off, and we thought we were so daring. Anyway . . ." She took a spoonful of salmon mousse. "It was a different time. Today, it's 'I want it, and I want it now.'"

"Are you going to Art Basel?" That's the question one hears up and down Madison Avenue in October and November.

Recently, I was having lunch with a public relations professional who puts together events for the annual Miami art confab. She explained how her clients go to parties while their consultants roam the fair, snapping iPhone photos.

"Sometimes they buy, but for the most part, they wait," she said, nibbling on her Nova and bagel.

"For what?" I asked.

"To see if someone else is interested," she said. "If this one or that one wants it or gives it the nod, then they'll pony up the money."

"And if not?"

"The key is everybody wants what everyone else wants."

"Which is?"

"That's part of the game, figuring out what everyone else wants."

"How do you do that?"

"To tell you the truth, there are, like, three guys deciding what everybody should buy," she whispered. "Three guys."

"Perhaps they all convene and decide at the diner," I offered.

A few days later, I was having breakfast with a good friend in his Madison Avenue aerie, where the morning sun illuminated the Greco-Roman sculptures, Renaissance paintings, Georgian silver, and midcentury Modern furniture.

"When I go to Art Basel, I don't see art collecting as much as I see competitive spending," he said. "I see the same people who thirty years ago were at Studio 54 who are still behind the velvet rope. Only now it's Art Basel, and the entrance fee to an A-list party is a hundred thousand dollars for a starter piece." He offered me a serving dish of gravlax on toast points.

"Does that get them the piece and the invite?"

"Generally both. I'm not sure they know what they're buying, but they want to be players, and they take a dealer or consultant's advice. It's like the *CliffsNotes* of the art world, and then they take the plunge."

"Do they do any research?"

"That's the thing about the art fairs. It's the big-box retailer of the art world. You go up and down, aisle after aisle. Of course, there are reputable dealers, but, if you asked the collectors whether they got a condition report on the piece or asked about *provenance*, they'd probably say, 'What's that?'"

Shortly after that conversation, I was in the sleek, spartan gallery of one of the most respected blue-chip dealers, who sat with beautiful posture in a Mies black leather chair.

"Thirty, forty years ago, people bought and built collections slowly. Many of the great collectors even paid over time," he told me. "They savored each piece, got to know and support the artists."

Now, he said, "they're having dinner at their new ten-thousand-square-foot loft and realize they need a collection. They're often very nice people in a hurry. And of course, they get the collector's bug and become insta-experts."

"As in?"

"My consultant is better than your consultant. This gallery is better than that one. And it's all backed with the insta-library. X linear feet of books on every artist. One cannot have the insta-collection without the insta-library," he observed.

"What's your take on the collections?" I asked directly.

"There is a greater possibility of seeing the piece back on the market."

"When?" I asked.

"After the insta-divorce." He offered the salmon roe sushi on a silver platter.

"Do you truly love that?" I asked a high-profile collector who was giving me the tour of his impressive renovations, as we came upon a controversial work that could certainly be deemed pornographic.

"It shocks. It unsettles," he said.

"Is it hard to live with?" I asked.

"I would find it harder to live with what some dealers call an 'over-the-sofa' piece," he said, mentioning an artist you see up and down the avenue in "starter" collections. "That would be more shocking to my sensibilities."

"But do you love it?" I pressed him.

"*Love* is a big word. All I can say is it's for sale. If someone offered me my number, I would take it." He shrugged. "Everything is for sale in my home, including my fiancée," he said, giving a lascivious look to the semiclothed nymphette who floated by.

"What do you say to the naysayers who don't approve of your artwork?" I ask.

"I have three things to say: They're just jealous. They can kiss my ass. Let them laugh—I'm laughing all the way to the bank."

In another conversation, my friend, one of New York's most influential, heralded architects, laughed ruefully at the state of the art scene as we ate alfresco on Houston Street. "I have never met more show-off wannabes," she said. "They're all full of shit. I have seen the entire arc from 1980s to 2013. I don't know if you know in the '80s I was an assistant to a great pop artist. I was in a micro-mini from Trash and Vaudeville."

"Really? What did you do?"

"I gessoed his canvases. I answered the phone. I was seventeen and hot." She paused. "I have always been connected to the artists. That's the big difference. My clients care about art first, beauty first, soul first."

"And the rest?"

"It's become only about money. And of course they get to slum it. You know it's about Bohemian Thursdays where they get to go to the studio. It's a conceit; it's become about vanity."

"More vino?" I offered.

"Of course. Your poached salmon looks divine."

I glanced across the restaurant and saw a young international art dealer caress his model girlfriend's leg under the table.

"I just bought [one of the great artists] for [a high-flying real estate person]," he said, virtually shouting, impressing the young girl.

"Do you want to go to Monaco for the weekend?" he added, stroking her leg carnally.

"I would love to," she replied.

"Come back with me. I have a great painting to show you," he said with a wolfish grin.

II.

ON THE PARK

4. I GET NO RESPECT, JUST THE BILLS

The Affluent Husband Is the Invisible ATM

ONE KNOWS THE SUMMER IS OVER when the pumpkins miraculously appear overnight on Hamptons farm fields. As orange is now a fashion color of choice associated with champagne, cashmere, and luxury brands, one would hope the startling array of orange globes would be an advertising stunt *or* for propping a set for a Movie of the Week on Pilgrims. Despite the summer heat, there they were, though, bursting in full glory as people were still making their way to the beach.

To prolong the summer-*ish* nights, my wife, Dana, and I journeyed downtown to meet Park Avenue Princess and friends at Miss Lily's for a repast of spicy jerk chicken and reggae-infused rum (Blackwell of course!). As the women caught up on back-to-school issues and fall schedules, the husbands all rehashed how quickly this particular summer had flown, not to mention their own familial concerns.

"It's the craziest thing, " Park Avenue Prince said. "I'm king in the office, but when I get home I get no respect." He looked slightly out of place, holding a Red Stripe instead of the ubiquitous glass of rosé I always see attached to his hand.

Real Estate Kingpin immediately echoed similar sentiments.

"I feel the same way. In the office it's 'Yes, sir,' to everything, but when I get home and walk through the door I become invisible." He sighed. "I'm the invisible ATM."

"I know how you feel. My daughter locks the door and when I knock on it, she tells me to go away," Park Avenue Prince declared.

"Why do you allow locks on the doors?" I asked in a stupefied manner.

"They were there. Even if I took out the locks, her standard line is 'Don't come in, I'm not dressed.' There's no barging in on that statement," he said wearily.

"Everyone is either studying, playing video games, or on social media. I'm 'ssshed' when the tutors are there and have to fend for myself for a drink or a meal when we don't have dinner plans."

"No one talks to me unless they want something," another husband groused.

"I know deep down there *is* appreciation, just no level of *service*," Real Estate Kingpin said.

"The best is when the kids or my wife take the driver and I have to hail a cab," Park Avenue Prince sighed. "Not that anyone would notice."

I am very often in the company of women, and I do get to hear more of my fair share of complaints about men. "Men," the ladies gripe, "are boorish, bossy, or difficult. They all have ADD, and/or are not nearly thoughtful enough." And the list goes on and on. Many of the men I know have a longer fuse when it comes to complaining or confrontation. That said, even for many of the men from the so-called happy, long-term marriages, there is a growing tendency to question the status quo. Many feel underappreciated, taken for granted, and only relegated to the role of provider. No one pays them any attention until someone "wants something." This reality, coupled with escalating bills and diminishing affection, causes a strange set of emotions. Fallout ranges from benign acceptance to a finely honed sense of humor to simmering rage. The result is that many an invisible husband and father start to look outside the marriage and family unit for some sort of validation. Hearing the man's perspective provides an unusual peek into both the male psyche and men's longing.

"I always had this suburban fantasy," the Old Westbury Private Equity Guy declared over lunch at Morimoto, "that I would come home and my wife would answer the door in high heels and an apron, offering me a freshly prepared martini." He laughed at the highly improbable thought.

"What is the real husband reality on the North Shore these days?" I asked as I negotiated the salmon roe with my chopsticks.

"Don't get me wrong; I love my wife, but the moment I walk in the door I'm told to 'do this and do that and did I do this or forget to do that.' I work hard all week, and then on the weekends I'm expected to pick up all the slack because my wife says she does it all week long. And she runs off to a doubles match or a spin class," he said without malice.

"So you feel the subject of the underappreciated husband threatens the equilibrium?"

"Absolutely. It's like the women band together and always want to blame the men for everything. 'He did this. He did that . . .'" He mock gesticulated.

"Do you think some of the women are unrealistic?"

"That's a great word. So many women I know just want, want, want without having to give."

"Do you think it's different living in Old Westbury?"

"I think the commute is longer—that said, I still don't think I'd be getting any more respect if I were living in the city."

"Your biggest complaint?"

"I don't understand where it says in the manual that if a wife is handling the kids during the week that I have to work double time over the weekend to relieve her. It would be different if we were doing it together."

"So do you talk about it?"

"Most men don't like confrontation. We're exhausted. How many times does a man start a verbal confrontation with a woman? The wives do all the time, but it's just too much effort."

"Another glass of sake?"

"You bet your ass."

"I think in any long-term marriage there is a complacency that comes with time. Everyone settles into that role, which is fine as long as you buy into it and you are secure." Southern Gentleman adjusted his collar stay. We were having a postsquash cocktail in a turn-of-the-century club's oak-paneled bar and he was filling me in on his divorce proceedings. And lawyer bills.

"Meaning what?" I toyed with the plate of anemic carrot sticks and blue cheese.

"Take something as simple as your spouse flirting. I never saw it as harmful. As an example, when things were going well, we hired a lacrosse coach for my son—they always have these great names like Trey or Vaughn—and he was a great-looking guy and he would come for lunch at the house et cetera."

"Was the flirting very overt?"

"I felt at the time it was harmless and she needed to feel good about her femininity. I was happy to be in the background. I think when you feel good and fulfilled, you don't question the sanity of the situation. You feel you're working together for the greater good."

"And?" I prompted, ordering another round.

"And when you are unfulfilled and not secure, then you start to question—being part of the supporting cast, for instance . . . and the flirting, of course."

"Then what happened?" I asked, knowing his *War of the Roses* divorce had set him back emotionally and financially for a number of years.

"When the divorce happened, I realized I greatly resented being the guy who just wrote checks and didn't get a huge amount of respect or attention. I now understand I was totally taken for granted. I have to admit I actually thought it was supposed to be that way." He shrugged.

"Why?"

"It was the way I was brought up." He smiled. "That was my father's life."

"Was he happy?" I said, looking at a framed nineteenth-century oil painting of a club president.

"Now I'm not so sure." He paused thoughtfully. "Maybe that's why he perfected a world-class martini."

I am not above eavesdropping and savoring a conversation as I am essentially a people watcher and have only come to understand, recently, that I am also a People Listener. I was at my usual spot at the bar in the divine Candle 79, perhaps the only restaurant on the Upper East Side that has a true Downtown sensibility. I was feasting on the supremely innovative vegan cheese plate (the culinary equivalent to a lap dance) when two standard-issue Wall Street types sat down on the high stools right next to me. Their conversation seemed tailor-made to this story.

"I am *sooo* done. It's like no one paid any attention to me for twenty years and now that the kids have gone off to college, she expects me to be with her every minute." The older of the two motioned broadly in his bespoke suit.

"That's normal. She's having her midlife crisis and wants to drag you into it," his friend said, scanning the menu.

"I have my own to worry about." The older man motioned the bartender. "I'll have a vodka. Make it a double."

"Me too," his friend added.

"And what's going on with you? How's Chantal (not her real name)?"

"She's so busy with the kids and her charity work, she has zero time for me. I used to think guys who cheated were bad guys—but I no longer condemn infidelity. I think the last time we [a vulgar phrase suggesting intimacy] was like six months ago."

"I mean, if a woman's not going to service her man, someone else will," he stated matter-of-factly.

They clinked glasses in a sober fashion.

"I'm so tired of the complaining and the excuses."

"Listen, I have the opposite problem. You still have kids in high school. Now that we're empty nesters, suddenly Nancy (not her real name) wants to go at it all the time. I'm handling it with pills, how about you?"

The younger of the two scanned the bar, looking over at the attractive blonde who was eating seitan alone. "Yeah," he said, catching her eye. "I just decided to outsource."

"It's so easy to be a blamer," Second Wife said over the phone. Dana had put her on speaker as we lay in our bed after watching the latest episode of *Homeland*.

"I think so much of it has to do with exhaustion," she continued.

"Exhaustion or lack of sleep?" I asked, looking longingly at the fluffy duvet.

"There's always so much to do: going to bed so late, the alarm going off at six, getting the kids off to school, getting them to their sports, doctors' appointments, social events, play dates, activities, getting my job at work done, working out, having a social life ourselves."

"I'm exhausted just hearing about it, but we have the same life. I could use some sleep right about now," I said; the clock read 12:50 a.m. At that moment my youngest daughter walked in, saying she was having trouble sleeping.

"That's ironic," I said.

"Let's face it," Second Wife said. "We will never sleep again until the kids go off to college. Just deal with it." She laughed ruefully.

"And the idea of the underappreciated husband? True or false?" I asked her before she hung up.

"All I can say is when my head hits the pillow I have *nothing left to give*."

"What about Steve (her husband)? Does he have a problem with that?" I asked.

"Problem? He went to sleep two hours ago."

A barbecue in September in the Hamptons is a wonderful thing to behold and as the gaggle of children gathered in the rec room to play table tennis and the women *ooh*ed and *aah*ed over one mother's newest arrival, the men gathered around the grill looking at the array of seared meats. There is always something primal about men and their grills. As the flames hit the meat, it seemed an opportune time to ask if there were any invisible husbands in this group.

"Being a master of the universe at work and a servant at home can be somewhat disconcerting," the host remarked on the fly. "You want the troops to stop when you walk in the door and just focus on you, and when it doesn't happen, it's always a bit of a letdown," he said to the other nodding fathers as he used his tongs skillfully. "Do you want your turkey burger medium or well done?" he asked.

"Well done," I said. "I'll take the rest in for the kids." We all peered at the perfect array of burgers and hot dogs he arranged on a platter. I took it into the kitchen, where a group of children of all ages were sitting at a round table conversing and happily mimicking the adults.

"Burgers and hot dogs here," I said cheerily. No one responded to my call for food.

"Would anyone like a burger or hot dog?" I tried again. "I'm here to serve." I said it in a joking but serious fashion.

Finally my son looked up from the table and said, "I'll have a burger, please."

"I'll have a hot dog, too," my older daughter said. I had a spring in my step as I took the platter over. In that moment I went from being a server to being useful to being needed—in a good way, where I wasn't just a check writer.

"Thanks, Dad," my son said as he looked up at me when I offered him the platter, and he took a burger and bun. "You're the best." He smiled brightly at me.

"Mom, isn't Dad the best!" he called out.

"Yes, there's no one like your dad," she echoed.

As he took the burger from the platter and thanked me, suddenly, despite the crazy schedule, the lack of sleep, and the overall stress of life, everything seemed to make complete sense. And I was *visibly happy*.

5. THE NEW DIVORCE IS NO DIVORCE

AS LUCK WOULD HAVE IT, the Silver Fox had invited me to join him at a retreat in Malibu, a sensational summer camp for adults that's a cross between a chic boutique hotel on the Amalfi Coast and the Betty Ford Center. Most people came without spouses (children don't watch themselves, you know), and it was a diverse group. I was struggling up an arid mountain peak when I began chatting with an attractive redhead from San Francisco. We exchanged pertinent information.

"Are you married or divorced?" I asked her as we both sipped water from our CamelBaks in the blazing sun.

"Neither," she said. "I am married, but I am separated. We live on the same property but have two different living areas. It's called nesting."

"Nesting?"

"Yes, we have children together and are best friends but we aren't divorced."

"So do you see other people?"

"Yes, in between family vacations."

On a subsequent trip to the left coast, I had lunch with Hollywood

Mogul at the Ivy in Santa Monica. He looked trim, wiry, and youthful as he bounded into the restaurant on two devices. (Everyone who is successful in LA looks like they are going to a Lakers game.)

"Our marriage may be dead, but our assets are very much alive," he said, spooning the espresso crema onto his tongue.

"I had a mentor when I first got into the movie business"—he mentioned a legendary producer—"He'd been married at that point, five or six times, and he said the best business advice he could ever give me was never to get divorced. Every time he got divorced he moved into a smaller and smaller house until he ended up in an apartment on the wrong side of the tracks."

"The sex went out of the marriage years ago," Hollywood Mogul went on without emotion, "but we're still best friends."

"How did you work that deal?" I asked, marveling at his alluring tuna tartare.

"She always enjoyed a much quieter life. Listen, I respect a woman who goes gray, but the net net is I don't want to have sex with a grandmother," he said, flashing high-wattage laminations at two young starlets sharing crab cakes at the next table.

He flexed his ageless bicep, licked his lips, and brandished his Patek as if part of the LA mating ritual.

"And where do you all live?"

"She lives in [a bedroom community of LA] and I live in the house (a gated mansion on *über*exclusive Los Angeles drive). Our girls divide their time when they are in LA and it makes total sense. I have no desire for more children and they're going to get it all anyway. This is the way the old money people do it. So much smarter. As far as I'm concerned, this part of my life is dedicated to fun, fun, fun."

"So you get together for the holidays?"

"Of course. My favorite time. Darlene (not her real name) makes the meanest turkey. If we had gotten divorced, she would have kept the stuffing recipe. For that alone, it's worth staying married. And this way I have the best excuse in the world when I'm dating."

"What's that?"

"I'm married so I never have to commit. Now, what's all this talk of divorce? Are you OK?"

"I always say I married my second wife first." I laughed.

"We're not separated, we only live separately," said Chic Euro Chick (a minor-titled noble from someplace we all like to go on vacation). She flicked her ash, sporting not one but two Buccellati cuffs, as we made our way into New York's Monkey Bar. She double-kissed those in charge and we were seated promptly.

"Do you live in different apartments?"

"No darling, in different wings," she confessed as she stashed her silver lighter in her chic Boxer bag. "In my opinion, that's the only way. We have breakfast and dinner together with the twins in the common area," she said. "And then we retire to our own wings. It's divine. Very Edwardian. I have my books, my Kindle. I have peace and quiet."

"Did divorce ever come up?"

"Divorce is so . . ." She struggled to find the English word. "So . . . bourgeois. People got divorced in my parents' generation. Look how that turned out."

The following week, I visited a leading clergyman who was recuperating from an illness across town in the well-stocked library of his sprawling West End Avenue apartment.

"If the option is either divorce or a deal, I prefer the latter," he said.

"You do?" I asked, somewhat surprised.

"Yes, of course," he said, offering me tea. "There is something to be said for family dinners, vacation time, and holidays. Divorce is a disaster for the children. Some never recover. The kids don't care if the parents are sleeping together or sleep in the same room. They care that they are both there when they wake up in the morning and go to bed at night. They just want everything to be OK.

"Sometimes people can't stay together and divorce is justified. But I always counsel people to stay together if they can," he went on. "I cannot tell you how many people I counsel who have separate bedrooms and lives. And they're the well-adjusted ones. It's different when people are unhappy in their twenties and thirties, but making a deal is a phenomenon for fifty-year-olds."

"And do you condone extramarital relationships?"

"I didn't say that. That's not my business, and who am I to judge? That said, if it comes down to a messy divorce with the parents at war, I honestly think this is a better solution."

"If you are young and don't have children, divorce is perfectly fine," the Seventh Avenue Kingpin declared over luscious gigande beans at the superb Yefsi Estiatorio.

"Is that why you stay together?" I asked, knowing he has his own deal with his long-term spouse.

"When you have children—and I also have grandchildren—divorce adversely affects a lot of people. I believe in this idea of the family unit. When you build a life together, you don't divorce your wife or your family because she might not be interested in sex anymore. Sex is not always the driving issue. In fact, I would rate it a distant third at a certain age.

"My children and grandchildren are my focus. I have friends who have gone through two- or three-year divorces. The damage is incalculable. And then the kids mostly hate all the new players who show up . . . It's a story as old as time. The kids, who are no longer kids at this point, are also afraid the parent is going to end up with someone inappropriate and change the will. Don't think I haven't seen that before, especially if the kids aren't as successful as the parents and are living off their largesse. And let's not forget some second wives can be more demanding and mercenary than the first one! That's trouble."

"Well, you know what I always say: where there's a will, there's a relative," I said.

He continued: "Imagine spending years and millions, suing each other—years of character assassination in court. For what? Because someone won't put up with the wife's trainer or the husband's stripper? The Europeans have it right. When the man wants to have a bit of fun, he buys the young lady a Hermès bag and off she goes. The wife gets the earrings from Graff; the bigger the indiscretion, the bigger the stone. They're not testifying against each other; they're smart. Think of all the eight-figure divorces."

"So did you say anything to your wife about the new deal?"

"Some people do and some people don't," he said, avoiding the question and looking at his Cartier tank. "The smartest women, in my opinion, turn a blind eye to keep the family together." He downed his espresso and waved good-bye.

He had an appointment to keep, but didn't mention with whom.

Part of the upper crust, fabulous interior designer Lily Whitebread and I were catching up over a scrumptious Nutella, fruit, and toast confection at the Eurosleek Artisan Boulanger. Witty, entertaining, and *très intéressante*, Lily lives the transatlantic lifestyle while her husband lives in and around Charleston, South Carolina.

"So do you ever see each other?" I asked.

"Hardly ever," she said, amused.

"Did you ever consider getting a divorce?"

"Why would I?" she asked without irony. "That's the beauty of it. He lives there, and I live all over. It's the only way to do it, dear. I call it Marriage 3.0."

"So you never see each other?"

"No. We do speak and collaborate over Charlotte (their grown daughter), and he sends flowers on my birthday and anniversary. Who wants to get divorced? Why disrupt your life? I see this as a new trend," she said, munching on a flaky brioche that apparently had no effect on her rail-thin figure.

"How so?" I raised my hand for more coffee.

"In the old days," she said, smiling, "people had the good grace to drop dead. Now everyone works out, eats well, and their cholesterol is under control. The men are living so much longer. So when the kids are grown, one is confronted with one's spouse."

"Did you actually sit down and work it all out?"

"There's no need to," she said, twirling her wedding band. "It just *is*."

"Do your friends have deals?"

"Some do and some don't. The really successful ones tend to. We don't need a man for anything."

"Then why be married?" I knew I was pushing Lily's white buttons.

"It's part of the fear that women have about not having 'Mrs.' in front of their names. Today, one has a choice. Marriage is a choice but not a mandate. Many women went charging into the workforce in my day and then bailed. If the husband lets them go spinning and lunching and shopping, many women would rather take that option.

"For me and my friends, speaking on the phone to our husbands and going off to the South of France or Siena for the summer couldn't be more wonderful. Brioche, dear?"

With Memorial Day fast approaching and the pleasures of seersucker and linen beckoning, I received a call from a Southern Gentleman I know through the squash circuit. He is going through a *War of the Roses*–style divorce.

"Up for a game and a martini afterward?" I asked.

"I'll take the martini but I haven't been playing lately. Things have been extremely difficult. We're actually going to trial next week," he said in a shell-shocked tone.

"Why don't you just split it down the middle and call it a day?" I asked.

"She's getting all sorts of bad advice from people who are telling her she should be getting more than I have. It's been disastrous. The only people who are winning are the lawyers."

"Yes, I have heard that before," I sympathized.

"These divorce lawyers are undertakers for the living," he moaned. "You lose a loved one and all your money. Not to mention I hardly see my children anymore."

"I am so sorry to hear that. Let's make plans for drinks at the club," I offered.

"That would be great," he said before hanging up. "If I could have martinis by intravenous, I would."

6. NEVER MIND THE NANNIES, DRIVERS ARE THE NEW DADS

LIVING ON THE UPPER EAST SIDE, one gets accustomed to seeing ridiculous things, from $300 plates of truffle pasta to couture dog collars. But this one was a first. The other evening, I was walking off the leaden canapés after another deadly fund-raiser in someone's "aerie." As I was passing a venerable Park Avenue residential building, a black SUV came to a halt.

A Dwayne Johnson–proportioned driver got out, lifted a supine teenager from the backseat like a bag of golf clubs, and lugged him to the door. "I've taken away your cell phone," he said. "You'll get it back when your parents return." He then deposited the drunken youth in the lobby. "Sleep next to a garbage can," he cautioned before leaving his charge in the custody of the doormen.

The *New York Post* recently wrote about parents who were passing off their classroom volunteer duties to nannies, much to the dismay of their private schools, or rather, of the other moms, who didn't fancy selling snickerdoodles alongside hired help at bake sales. The story ricocheted around the Upper East Side, a neighborhood whose privileged parents stand accused of outsourcing every child-rearing task, from cooking to etiquette training.

As someone who lives and raises kids there, I'm here to tell you that these charges are all pretty much true. (It's actually worse.) But now drivers are stepping in as parents as well? That was something I hadn't heard.

I don't want to be seen as a hypocrite here; we use car services during the week and occasionally a driver on the weekend as needed. But let me be clear that these are people who merely transport our family—nothing more—and there's always another adult in the vehicle. As my kids get older, will I be calling upon these men to mete out punishments to my children? Ground them? Attend parent-teacher conferences in my stead? Drop them off at college someday?

I'm sure it's been done before.

The next day, I was having drinks at the kind of private club that still insists on ties, no jeans, and no technology (a port in the storm when you are surrounded by private equity guys), when I relayed the incident to a friend with older children. He explained that to a growing degree, drivers are the eyes and ears of Uptown parents: protecting, chaperoning, disciplining, and dragging teens out of clubs when they are wasted.

Crucial to these drivers' job success is being able to finesse the tension between parents who hire them to spy on their children and teenagers who try to ditch their captors at every turn. "Ex-cops and detectives make the best drivers," my friend said. "They are good at picking up clues, and they get right in there and pull the kids out of clubs when they're shitfaced. Must be a Staten Island thing."

"Aren't the parents supposed to do that?" I asked, sipping the kind of martini that only a gentile club could make.

"Of course." He munched on an olive. "When they're back from St. Barths."

"As far as I'm concerned, it was either a driver or boarding school," said a friend the next night. My wife, Dana, and I were out with another couple who are big in real estate banking. Their kids are five years older than our own, and their driver's job duties are as limitless as their kids' run of the city.

"If you think I'm going to police my children after midnight, you have another thing coming. Until I got Vince, I was missing spin at seven thirty," she said. "It was starting to affect my looks."

This is a mom who started letting her kid drink in front of her at age fifteen. "They were coming home drunk . . . so now I let them have wine or beer in front of me," she said, knocking back a vodka and cranberry.

"At fifteen?" Dana asked.

"You'll see when your kids get to be our kids' ages," she said. "Younger wives are always so idealistic until the moment comes. And then you'll fold like the rest of us."

The more I asked, the more the stories began to pile up, many of them of a cat-and-mouse nature. Parents hiring ex-Mossad agents with spy cams and installing tracking devices in their kids' phones (until the kids were smart enough to disable them). Children running out the back door of a club to party down the street while the driver slept out front.

A golfing partner revealed that his family's driver, an ex-cop, carries a Glock. "I'd rather have a driver that my kids know and like than have them take cabs from someone right off the boat. Who knows if they're safe?" he said, swinging his sand wedge in the trap. "It's accountability. And that matters to me." (Also, if there's a traffic altercation, having an ex-cop call the cops can't be the worst thing.)

A college-age man I know—who still speaks twice a month to the driver his family hired for him when he was in high school—said that having a driver had its advantages when it came to high school romance. Except when he was dating a girl whose family had one as well.

"Her father would send her driver to follow us to see what was going on. Of course, we tried to lose the tail."

"Did it work?"

"Sometimes, but he was good. He always managed to track us down."

Last year, when my son wanted to take a cab with a friend to a Downtown party at nine p.m., I vetoed it, thinking twelve was a little on the young side. The other child went. I'm still surprised by other parents' willingness to give their teenagers the run of the city and leave the drivers in charge. When it comes to going out unsupervised to parties and clubs, thirteen is the new eighteen. Why not keep it simple and put the kids on a shorter leash?

As it turns out, there is no single answer. There are the "me time" parents, who complain that family time or chaperoning their kids puts a dent in their own social lives. Then there are the divorced couples, who rely on drivers as neutral shuttle services between both homes, with the driver deployed as communicator and mediator. In my observation, divorces often breed permissiveness, because the parties can't agree on a uniform parenting style.

The last subset—perhaps the chief offenders—is a group whose own deficiencies as teenagers fuel their kids' social lives. They're the formerly uncool high school students who want desperately to live vicariously through their children. The men tend to be Napoleonic, and, having conquered the world of finance, they often have unlimited cash and credit to dispense to their progeny. They populate New York campuses with incredibly indulged and well-dressed children and believe that money and power are the keys to popularity. For them, drivers are less chaperones than enablers: helping kids gain club access, bottle service, fake IDs, and, yes, romantic partners.

Of course, all this late-night surveillance comes at a cost. I was at a charity gala in the Met's Egyptian wing when I ran into one of the Upper East Side Queens of Consumerism, noted for her outsize diamonds as well as her outsize handbag collection. "Weekend drivers all want premium pay after eight," she lamented, clicking a crystal minaudière in the shape of a farm animal. "And pizza's not good enough. They want spicy tuna rolls and black cod with miso takeout." She touched up her lips and floated off like a chiffon-and-diamond nimbus cloud.

And why shouldn't drivers want Nobu? All the better to nourish them for long nights babysitting the misbehaving offspring of the city's elite.

Some may argue that there is a moral lapse in letting the driver take on parenting duties. My kids are still too young, so I leave it to others to judge. But would a little help with algebra be out of the question?

7. NEED AN INTERN WITH A STRONG SENSE OF ENTITLEMENT AND BAD MANNERS? HIRE A RICH KID

VERY FEW PEOPLE KNOW how to throw a good party, let alone ever host one. Or even know *how* to entertain.

I learned the basics when I was my fraternity's social chairman in college and came to understand how much hard work and planning go into a memorable evening.

Social Powerhouse's *Playboy*-themed party in the Hamptons was among the summer's best.

Perhaps it was the half-naked PYTs frolicking in the custom grotto, the myriad of bunnies on high-wire trapeze-style swings, the muscled shirtless models in bow ties, the famous '80s singer, or the convincing bathrobed Hefner look-alike. It was *Gatsby* style and a rarity.

I was standing under a festooned big top, conversing with Big Brother (the famous adman/TV host), with whom I have a close, long-standing relationship, when the twentysomething son of an acquaintance interrupted our conversation, as if we were peers.

"How do you two . . ." He made the hand motion indicating knowing each other.

"I used to work for him when I first entered the business, before starting my first firm," I said.

"No, we worked together," Big Brother said graciously.

"No, I worked for you, but that's kind." I laughed. "And before that I was a receptionist."

The young person looked at me in wide-eyed horror.

He trailed me to the bar. "Richard, why do you let people know that you were a receptionist?"

"Working your way up is respectable," I said. "The most successful people in Hollywood worked their way up in the CAA mailroom, as an example."

"Maybe," the be-Rolexed millennial said. "But I'd rather work my way up from the top."

There is a rampant disease today that goes beyond borders. Entitlement is a contagious, insidious state of mind that has infected a whole generation of young people who feel they deserve things based on who they think they are or who their parents are. Or who they've been told they are.

Entitlement also afflicts adults, who feel they should have or get things based on their friends having them or just feeling worthy. It's hard to pinpoint the derivation of where and when the disease started, but it's an epidemic.

"Mr. Kirchenbaum, I am very disappointed that you do not have a position for me," proclaimed the e-mail from a friend-of-a-friend's daughter, whom I did the favor of meeting for an informational interview. Besides misspelling my name, she wrote she found it *discouraging* that I let her know trying to secure an internship or job is best done in December, not two weeks before college graduation . . . that most internships had been filled six months earlier (as was ours) and that, since masses of graduating college seniors would be seeking jobs, it was not exactly the most ideal or opportune time. She picked up her Balenciaga bag at the news and left in a huff.

The next day the imperious e-mail arrived, my friend cc'd as if to apply further pressure.

Poor, long-suffering Carol, my assistant, has put up with years of rude and demanding behavior from "the children of" . . . with calls like "I'm in town and can meet him this week at three," or parents who call about an internship status grilling, "Does Richard KNOW that Bettina has not heard back yet?" "Don't they KNOW who SHE IS?" or "who WE ARE?"

I do like helping and encouraging young people. There is often a jewel who redeems the process, along with some well-raised and respectful children. That said, the majority do not send thank-you notes, even upon securing a coveted internship or job per my recommendation.

"The parents of," who can solve their children's every problem, desire, and whim with a black card, often do not know that entry-level jobs are a rarity and internship programs at large agencies have been cut for budgetary reasons.

I have Carol send each parent who asks this favor a *WSJ* article titled "Where Did All the Entry Level Jobs Go?" to give them a sense of reality and a preliminary education.

Unless of course the parents buy an internship at a school or charity auction. I often see the progeny of the rich nonchalantly rattle off working for the world's most famous movie producers and couturiers like they went to Friendly's for a Fribble.

"Yeah"—the high school junior cracks his gum—"last summer I was an assistant director for [world-famous Academy Award– winning director]." I have seen and heard it all. I particularly enjoy it when the interns flee their posts early for Saint-Tropez, thus bailing on their final presentations.

"I have, therefore I am owed," BFF therapist revealed over dinner at the Palm. This childhood bestie and I bemoan the sad state of affairs over creamed spinach and hash brown potatoes.

"Money and privilege are often a catalyst for this sprouting," she noted.

"How so?" I asked, eyeing the delectable fried onion rings.

"Take the whole trophy culture," she said. "The programs we send our children to are so expensive they all get a trophy just for being there. Kids expect ongoing trophy treatment, trophy lives." She sliced the strip steak.

"Not to mention trophy wives. Is it an issue in your practice?" I cut the glistening chicken Milanese.

"Yes, it's just another social ill like bullying or stealing."

"The root?"

"It's often a mask for insecurity, anxiety, uncertainty. It may be a Band-Aid for hopelessness, loss of control, or just a temporary elixir for fleeting happiness. The source differs from person to person but can be borne out of a parent's need to please. *No* is not a part of the vernacular. This may be a result of newfound wealth or parents who resolved never to say no to their children. The idea being that the more one says yes, the better the parent is."

"And what happens?"

"The outcome can be disastrous . . . Those whose needs are not met can become depressed, rageful, and often turn to substances."

"Or one can turn to food. Do you think our needs would be met if we ordered the Lyonnaise potatoes?"

"It starts as early as nursery school," L'actrice confided at the Watermill beach soiree. "The money and favors just to get into a school—it gets worse with each grade." A bikini-clad waitress hovered, presenting a tray of charcoal-fired lamb chops, which my companion politely declined.

I was seated on a white leather couch on the beach (what constitutes a Hamptons picnic) conversing with the Silver Fox's paramour, L'actrice. A formidable woman, she has raised substantial children and has been through the entire New York City private school process.

"You're dealing with crazy behavior. Five-thousand-dollar bottle service tables in the tenth grade." She shrugged.

"Don't you think that's a bit old nowadays, to start with bottle service?" I joked.

"When you don't give your children limits and there are no boundaries, they will either end up in jail for white-collar crime or in rehab. My friend's child is in rehab for the fourth time. When they have unlimited credit cards and access to everything, there is a reckoning." A waiter in only a bathing suit walked over offering Caribbean shrimp, which we waved away.

I spied a married woman in a metallic bikini chatting it up with the model/actor/surfer/bartender behind the bar. "You can't make your children's lives perfect and clean up every mess. If you hand your children a life they haven't earned, they think the rules don't apply to them."

"Salmon on the bar-b?" the waitress offered.

"Filet mignon skewers? Sliders with remoulade?" another cater waiter asked.

We both shook our heads no as my friend reached into her Dior for her BluePrintCleanse.

"There are people who want to give their children everything they didn't have . . . to be their children's friend or buy them popularity. Or they're not around enough and bribe them with money."

"Hot dogs? Lobster roll?"

"Sometimes you just have to say no."

"The new money prefers to live in splendid isolation." Jonny Van der Klump, who hails from a Midwest fortune, swept the blond lock off his forehead at the club his great-grandfather helped found.

"In my great-grandfather's day, great wealth was largely commodity and manufacturing based. Because the workers and the tasks were physical there was interaction. I remember when I went to the company Christmas parties as a child. I saw how many people my family was responsible for. I was taught to have a middle-class perspective, which is why I'm so frugal."

"Is that different today?" I tickled my martini's green olive with the swizzle stick.

"Great fortunes are being created through technology and finance, and there is little or no contact with workers, customers. One isn't held accountable for bad behavior. Many wealthy exist in a cosseted ether. They live protected lives in luxury and don't have to come in contact with the average person, adding up to a sense of unreality, the idea that the world exists for them and owes them what they want when they want it."

"And your children?"

"They have good manners. It starts with how one treats the waitress."

"Or taking an ill-behaved child out of the restaurant."

"Some parents have no control over the basics."

"Did you feel entitled growing up?"

"I felt I had a responsibility to serve. Not to be served," he said, thanking the waiter profusely.

"When someone under the age of eleven asks you if you are flying private or commercial, you know things are out of hand."

"That cannot be true." I coughed.

I was at Sant Ambroeus with Jannsen (not his real name), an art dealer who resides in Europe.

"But it is." He sipped his Negroni. "It was a client's son. He wanted to know how I was getting to Miami Art Basel. When I told him that I was on Delta, he said, 'Catch a ride with us.' I was floored. I am not used to being invited on a G-4 by someone who comes up to my belt loop. What's next? Lighting up a Cuban in his Volcom hoodie? Very inappropriate."

"Did you say that?" I asked him.

"Richard, these people are my clients. My parents brought us up to be seen and not heard. In those days, money had rules. One didn't flash it around. Today it's all about competitive cash. Anyone with a few dollars expects all the accoutrements because they can throw a few Benjies on the table. It's total money anarchy."

"And how many of these people are your clients?"

"Ninety percent," he said wistfully. "But don't print that unless you disguise me."

I battled the traffic on 27 to make it on time to the fund-raiser in Southampton. A dear friend was being honored at one of the turn-of-the-century estates. I respect his work ethic, big heart, good nature, and philanthropy and wanted to show up on time. I found him surrounded by his loving family and myriad others praising him on the honor.

As I gave him a hug and congratulated him, he mentioned his hardscrabble roots and how lucky he was to be able to give back.

"It's due to your hard work, your vision, and your business ethic. And your amazing wife," I offered.

"Thank you," he mused. "So what's your next article on, Richard?"

"I'm doing a piece on entitlement. Thoughts?"

"Yes," he offered immediately. "I always say I wish I had my children's upbringing, and I wish they had mine," he said as he was called to the stage.

I couldn't have agreed more as I thought of my own family. With that, the chocolate mousse was served.

III.

UPTOWN PROBLEMS

8. DATING TIPS FOR UPTOWN DIVORCÉES

Middle-Aged Millionaires Just Aren't That into You

I WAS AT MY USUAL BANQUETTE TABLE at Cipriani catching up with my dear friend and fellow gala charity chair, the Impossibly Blond and Glamorous Socialite. She looked up, over her grilled salmon and leeks.

"Do you have anyone for my friend Leanne? Her divorce just became final."

I recalled a lithe brunette who looked good in Lilly, making the rounds of the Hamptons charity cocktail circuit along with her pint-size now-ex-husband.

"Is she realistic yet?" I asked.

"I think so."

"Good." I sipped my Bellini.

My friend and I, while an unlikely matchmaking duo, have been informally setting up divorced friends and "children of" on the Upper East Side for years, and with solid results. We always say we should charge a commission for our dating service, but that temptingly profitable idea would be too déclassé.

Our biggest challenge, time and again, is matching up middle-aged divorcées in the "pre-realist" stage, who have not realized that they have a choice of sex, money, or a warm body—but not all three in the same package.

"How did she make out in the divorce?" I asked my friend.

"All I know," she revealed, "is that the husband made her include her Birkins as a part of the settlement." She added: "At the *current* retail price." *Bien sûr!*

"She most likely will want the money, then." I paused, Rolodex-ing in my head the range of the newly wed and nearly dead. As I gave the hand signal for the check, I thought of a few years' divorced friend who could use a chatelaine for his manor, and Leanne was an ideal prospect.

"Oh yes, I think I have a good old-fashioned septuagenarian billionaire in Palm Beach for her. Not exactly scintillating, but his real estate portfolio has a personality all its own."

"Perfect," she said. "I'll call her with the good news."

A few years back, I cowrote a fairly well-known relationship book for women called *Closing the Deal*; the premise was that two married men's advice could help turn single women into *deal closers*. While we had no formal training as relationship experts, we just implicitly understood that if women understood men better, they'd have a better shot at closing the deal. Knowing your audience is always key, whether personally or professionally, and we offered advice on topics from hygiene to foreplay.

Where most rich divorcées fail is in assuming they can replace their husbands with a newer model pretty much like the old one. Sorry to say, this tends not to be the case. Most of the time, the divorced well-to-do male is not looking for his equal, but rather for a sexretary from the Midwest, preferably without an opinion. As one recently divorced hedge funder told me: "Being married to a smart, opinionated woman is work! Now I just want tits on a stick, a blond wig, and someone to tell me I'm great when I get home."

Women who take a tough line often wind up lonelier for it. At a political fund-raiser, my wife, Dana, and I were chatting with a well-regarded financier's ex-wife, who clearly exhibited pre-realistic dating tendencies. She laid out her requests like the Marshall Plan:

"My age or younger. I won't date a geezer. Richer—the richer the better. Sexy. OK, let's just cut to the chase: my ex if he had abs and a personality."

"Don't you think you shouldn't have a list?" Dana asked innocently.

"That's for *other* people," she snapped.

She is still on the prowl.

Far more successful are those who focus on just one wish-list item, for instance sex. Assuming the woman is not completely devastated, pulling a Mrs. Robinson is a popular rebound maneuver once the lawyers have retreated and the paralyzing legal battle becomes a bitter memory.

Seducing younger men works out well for one rock star's ex-wife I know, who prefers bedroom sizzle over an eight-figure net worth. Over lunch at Da Silvano, she professed to not care about money, which apparently is a British thing. (Not that she doesn't have an unlimited budget for couture.)

"I'm English," she said. "We don't *like* money. It's vulgar, never to be discussed."

"So you're not interested in a man with money?"

"Not at all. I'm into spontaneity. The younger the better, twenty-five to thirty. It's a win-win. They're in awe."

"Of . . . ?"

"My experience."

Notable hookups for such divorcées include affairs with French or Italian baristas, a Roman Casanova who preys on the newly divorced (despite good tailoring, he's overcommitted and overdrawn), and the occasional Moroccan rug salesman. ("She got a ride on his flying carpet!")

More common are the standard-issue service-industry providers: the omnipresent trainer, manny, male *or* female yoga instructor, Hamptons carpenter, contractor, driver, plumber, beach club attendant (for real Mrs. Robinson cred), and tennis pro. Since trainers are allowed an all-access pass to the family compound, they frequently help their clients lift and separate in different areas during the a.m. and p.m.

"Why is the trainer the obvious choice?" I asked a leading member of the clergy who confirmed the trend.

"I think it's accessibility and availability," he said. "If there's a man close by, it's affirmation, and it's exciting for them. I have seen women relatively happy for a period in this arrangement."

When finances aren't important—but sex isn't either—another option is "the warm body," a common choice among the older set that also has its appeal for the career woman.

The warm body tends to be the straight man's version of a walker: he may be dull as a month-old razor, but he provides an audience, especially to women who really want to do all the talking.

"Having a companion is nice. I already took care of a man once before," a Madison Avenue matron remarked, opening her Bottega Veneta wallet and plucking out her ATM card. "Dinner, a movie, a cruise, prop him up in a chair, and away we go." She smiled. "He doesn't say much, but I find he hangs on my every word."

Even younger women agree. "I just need him to change a light-bulb now and again," said a friend.

"Sex?" I asked.

"Whatever." She shrugged.

Not every divorcée, of course, is in a financial position to while away her days with the cabana boy (or his friendly, benign father), and some must resort to mercenary tactics to avoid expulsion from the golden triangle of Park Avenue, Sagaponack, and St. Barths.

"I wake up in a cold sweat that I'm only going to be able to afford a *white* brick building on Fifty-Seventh Street or a four-bedroom in the Financial District," my wife's friend lamented outside spin class. "Getting divorced is bad enough; the real estate downgrade is the final straw."

Contrary to popular misconception, just divorcing a rich man doesn't necessarily leave one set for life. I put a call in to an old friend who has a reputation as one of New York's toughest divorce attorneys. One of his three assistants put me through.

"You next?"

"Sorry to disappoint," I joked. After brief pleasantries, he told me business was booming now that couples can almost afford to part ways, and he laid out the economics.

"OK, let's be clear; if the woman has the real money in the relationship, she can do whatever she likes." That said, that's not *most* women.

"So let's just say you're a relatively affluent couple in the twenty- to twenty-five-million range. By the time the lawyers take their eight-figure slice and the mortgages are paid off when the residences are sold, she might end up with a six- or eight-million-dollar check. It sounds like a lot of money, but that's it for her, unless she marries again. A conservative three percent on six million—one hundred and eighty thousand dollars a year—is her clothing allowance from her former life."

"So then what happens?"

"The ones with younger kids get alimony and child support. But the smart ones end up with the best sixty-year-old they can find."

"And if they don't?" I asked.

"There's always Boca Raton," he said.

I was heartened to hear one last and affirming category surfacing above Fifty-Seventh Street. These are the women who, empowered by divorce, want a real relationship centered around their kids.

A leading divorce consultant (a businesswoman who acts like a general contractor for people going through the process) had this to say: "There are those women who want a man to take care of them. Then again, there are those women who say, 'I can do this,' and just want a nice, normal guy who loves kids. Someone to provide their children with a moral compass."

"So how do people meet guys like that?" I asked. "Do they fly coach or business instead of first?"

"If they start working again, they might meet them in the office, or at a kid's baseball game, for example. There *are* healthy relationships out there," she said. "From what I've seen, the women who get jobs afterward meet better men than the ladies who continue to lunch."

I have one successful female friend who met and married a very nice family guy who was moderately successful himself. The one prerequisite was a makeover: better shoes, a nice belt, and no dad jeans.

I was getting the financial papers on Sunday on Lexington Avenue when I ran into an acquaintance, a high-end real estate broker who specializes in white shoe co-ops; he was listing an exclusive Park Avenue 12 with southern exposure.

"It just came on the market. You know death and divorce are the best things about real estate in this city," he said darkly.

"Whose apartment is it?"

He mentioned a high-profile couple who had recently split.

I remembered the fabulous layout. "She doesn't want it?" I asked.

"She can't afford to buy him out."

"Too bad."

"I know. If she's smart, she'll get down to business and land an oligarch for papers," he joked. "You know some of these women are like the real estate themselves. They come on the market, too many showings, sit too long without a bid, and then the product gets burned."

Luckily, no such fate awaits two newly minted and very eligible divorced people I introduced in February at our annual Valentine's Day Jazz Brunch, where we served up a torch singer and made-to-order omelets to a variety of guests. Both parties have interesting careers, in addition to having children.

"You two should know each other." I literally hip-checked the lanky European businessman into view of my friend, a lovely entrepreneur. A friendship and fireworks ensued. Perhaps they had the advantage of finding each other when they were both considered fresh listings, new to the market, in prime Fifth and CPW locations. They snapped each other up.

A thank-you text appeared on my phone just yesterday revealing summer plans for the new couple: first a romantic trip to Anguilla, then two weeks in Cap Ferrat. Not only is love in bloom on two continents, but the very best thing is that in spite of it all, they won't have to move to Florida.

9. THE HIGH FLIERS

Uptown Pill-Poppers Struggle to Hide Excesses from the Kids

SPRING BREAK FOUND US fleeing manhattan for the glorious Los Angeleno sunshine, palm trees, and alfresco lunches by the Beverly Hills Hotel pool. We were ensconced in the famed Howard Hughes bungalow, which I am sure has withstood its own share of vibrations over the years. Still, nothing prepared us for the 4.9 earthquake that interrupted our reverie and shook us out of bed at 6:30 a.m. Like a fool I called the front desk for confirmation. "Yes, Mr. Kirshenbaum. That was indeed an earthquake."

The next day, after a sleepless night, we ran into myriad New York families, all on spring break, having McCarthy salads by the pool, fiddling with the romaine and cheddar. "Aftershocks can be worse than the quake," I worried aloud to anyone who would listen.

"Don't worry," my friend's platinum blond wife said, retrieving her pillbox, implants immovable in her string bikini top. As her toddlers pranced about, she opened what seemed like a veritable pharmacy in her designer clutch.

"A little Xany will do you good," she said, picking around in the compartments. "Let's see, I have Valium, Xanax. Oh, those are the antidepressants. Wait, are those the Klonopin or the Zoloft . . . ?" she pondered.

"A cosmo and Molly and you won't remember a thing," she offered. "Even if the big one comes."

Having grown up in the "Just Say No" generation, afflicted by fear, guilt, and propaganda, it's strange to see so many New York parents smoking, popping, and snorting as soon as their kids are counting sheep.

"It's the '80s again," a good friend said at a recent party, inhaling a funny cigarette and passing it along.

"Why's that?" I said, taking in the duplex transformed into a dance party.

She gesticulated above the din and deejay spinning electronic dance music. "Let's say you're at a party and it's a five. By smoking or drinking you already elevate it to a six or a seven. Time is valuable. All I have to say is: *elevate your party level for better times, baaaby.*"

"Well, *they* certainly are," I said, pointing to two married women (to men) I knew who were gyrating and making out in the corner.

"That's my point. You don't feel old, you feel free. You're having a renaissance," she said as she toked.

"Any downside?" I said, taking a Jell-O shot.

"I haven't heard any bad reviews." She shrugged in her vintage Halston halter. "Honestly, I want to go out there and have a great time. I want to be wasted, entertained. I just want to fly high and have fun. Take the edge off," she mused.

"The cause for all this fun?" I probed like a proctologist.

"It's a midlife crisis. Lots of *rich girls* doing coke, Mollys, and edibles behind their husbands' backs."

"And your husband?" I asked, wondering what the straitlaced banker would think.

"We don't have that kind of relationship," she said. "I'm honest."

"Honest?"

"I said to him, you're missing out. If you want to go out and have to deal with all these people *unmedicated*, that's your issue."

After I got back from LA, I was catching up with a friend after his family's ski trip to Aspen.

"How was your trip?" I asked.

"Half of New York was there," he said. "It was a crazy party."

"How was the skiing?" I asked.

"Everyone in Aspen was high. They were bumping off trees on the mountain like pinball machines. You cannot believe the dispensaries out there. By the end of the trip, the whole town was sold out. People were bringing back the infused gummy candies by the garbage-bag full."

"Are you serious?" I asked.

"People were eating those gummies like sunflower seeds. They were whacked."

"What do you think about it all?"

"Look," he said, asking his assistant to bring him a double espresso, "it's people trying to hang on to their youth. You can get wasted when you're in your forties and fifties but it's kind of sad when you see people in their sixties who are sloppy. So you might as well do it while you've still got it going on."

Our first weekend back from the left coast saw us at a dinner party in an elegant Normandy pile in Greenwich. It was a well-heeled and conservative crowd, which prompted me to ponder whether drug usage had made its way to suburbia. My dinner partner, a vivacious and convivial gal, seemed taken aback by my line of questioning.

"No. None of my friends do drugs here," she said with distaste. "They only drink. I think New York is just a faster crowd." She eyed me suspiciously as she took a spoonful of crème brûlée.

"I'm sorry, I didn't mean to offend you and ask if you were partaking. It's just that I am writing an article."

"Yes, I've read some of your pieces. You seem to know the most ridiculous people."

"That I do." I smiled.

"Wait." She turned to me in a discreet fashion, as if offering up the tidbit like a peace sign. "I think I have something for you. Do you know how all these women stay so thin?" she whispered, as if giving up the secret location to the Maltese falcon.

"How?" I leaned in.

"They take their children's ADD medication. It's all speed, suppresses the appetite."

"I was sober for a decade," a fellow charity board member and fairly new acquaintance revealed over lunch at Bill's. "My drinking was honestly the cause of my first divorce."

"First?"

"I've also been married multiple times. Runs in the family."

He asked the waiter for a whiskey, neat. "My mother was an artist, a socialite, an alcoholic, and, honestly, a drug addict. I was shipped off to a different boarding school with each new husband. That said, she had great style."

"All those schools," I sympathized. "That must have been difficult."

"It's all a blur between the beer and the bong hits."

"Do you and your friends still do drugs?"

"Well, everyone on the North Shore and in Palm Beach is friendly with the drink. Drinking is part of the culture—cocktails before dinner, roadies at the [*über*exclusive North Shore golf club], bloodies at the [fortresslike Palm Beach private club]."

"So no drugs?"

"Let's just say I'm trying to *teach* myself to do coke more. I bought a spoon."

"Teach yourself? Why?"

"I've gained so much weight from the beer and vodka, I'm starting to resemble a keg."

The next week, I met a golf buddy at Sant Ambroeus for a fluffy egg white omelette and espresso. As we were catching up, he said that his twelve-year-old son had walked into the apartment unannounced and smelled the marijuana.

"That's not cigarette smoke. Is that what I think it is? That's *illegal, Dad*!!!"

My friend tried to explain that adults sometimes relax in other ways.

"Who are you buying this from?" the son lectured. "These are bad people. Dad, do you want to go to JAIL?" he pleaded.

A similar story was relayed to me as well when a friend's daughter came home early and caught my friend, a conservative Madison Avenue private equity guy, smoking weed. The daughter shrieked, "Dad, what are you doing?" The father turned white and said—and I quote: "It's not mine, I'm just holding it for a friend."

The digital landscape has transformed everything, from book and food delivery to drug delivery.

"In college I used to have to go to some grungy park and meet 'the guy,'" said one of New York's high fliers. "Now it's just a text away. It's like when I first moved to New York and I could order in moo shu chicken. I thought having a doorman and ordering in takeout was the ultimate luxury. Now I'm getting the weed delivered to my doorstep. It's the next level of delivery!"

"I felt that way about Fresh Direct a few years back," the wife interjected, "and our dealer is very stylish. You should see, he's all in Dolce. In fact, I asked him where he got his blazer and told him to pick one up for Mark (not his real name) in a size forty-two."

"Oh, I love that blazer. I didn't realize it was from Yves (not his real name)."

"Now he's adding personal shopping as an extra service," she said admiringly.

"I have a different theory," Respected Uptown Therapist revealed in his office. *Why do they all love Danish Modern furniture with nubby fabric?* I wondered.

"There's an enormous amount of social pressure in New York City. To be thin, to be beautiful, to be rich and successful." He stroked his Freudian goatee. "There's a term, 'relative deprivation.'"

"Meaning?"

"You may have it all but you are relatively deprived compared to someone who has much more than you have. And then it's about appearances."

"I call it the press release," I offered. "Don't forget everyone has perfect children as well who are all *geniuses* and *savants*."

"With all this pressure, the drugs, drinking, and partying are the pressure valves. The more pressure, the more need for release."

"Perhaps that's why it's happening more in New York City?"

"It is undeniable that it is more stressful in the city. When you're doing drugs, you forget your problems. I see a lot of wives doing drugs to escape their husbands' reduced bonuses."

"Sounds like high school all over again."

"Yes. Even down to the rich popular kids. Only now they're parents."

Just this week I woke up in wrenching pain and headed to the dentist.

"You have a fractured tooth and it needs to come out. Most likely you'll need an implant."

I always say toothache is as bad as heartache, but not nearly as romantic.

"Give me *every* painkiller you have," I begged. "I also have a business function at six I have to attend." First came the Novocain, then the crushed Triazolam, then the gas. Two hours later I awoke, numb and swollen and still flying.

"I have one question," I asked the staff as they helped me to the waiting room. "Do you think it's OK if I make the cocktails? I have a few people I want to see."

"I think it's OK but don't overdo it," they stressed.

Dana was in the waiting room and steadied me to the car.

"I really think we need to go home," she said.

"Absolutely not," I protested, even though I was a bit unsteady. "I feel great."

When we got to the Lever House, we entered the party, Dana holding me by the elbow.

"Hi, Richard. So good to see you," the socialite said. "You look amazing. So relaxed."

"It's true," the editor agreed. "He looks ten years younger. No frown lines."

What would have been a nice but obligatory cocktail party seemed to pass in a flash with laughs and effervescent conversation. Indeed, I had elevated my party level.

That is, of course, until I woke up bleary-eyed, the next morning.

"Daaaad." My teenage son tugged at my blanket, as I lay supine in bed. "I really think you need to stay in this evening and get some rest. Enough is enough."

10. PAID FRIENDS

Weary of Genuine Relationships, Rich New Yorkers Hire Stand-Ins

LAST MAY, AS THE CHERRY BLOSSOMS transformed Central Park into a confectioner's dream, Dana and I accepted an invitation to a charity gala from an international couple who maintain a residence in New York. While we see them only occasionally, our interaction, though intermittent, has been consistent, and we have become acquainted with their close circle of friends.

Museum galas can be as dusty as medieval tapestries, but this particular evening the great room sparkled. As we made our way to their table, we saw an eclectic mix of the usual suspects: their obsequious decorator, a silent banker from Monaco, and the wife's LA-based stylist and couturier. Noticeably absent was the couple's omnipresent and soigné art consultant, who always seemed to be the chatty third wheel.

As I turned to the hostess over the tuna tartare and avocado and complimented her acorn-size emerald earrings, I asked where the advisor was, having seen him cohost virtually every event.

"We had a falling-out," she said, misty-eyed.

"That must be upsetting," I offered. "I know how close you were."

"Yes. I considered him to be one of my dearest friends."

"What happened?"

"It was a billing issue," she said, sniffling.

"Billing?"

"He usually charges fifteen percent on the art he brought us," she whispered in near grief, "but we found he was also charging us on things we found at auction, and my husband had to let him go."

Early in September, Dana and I saw those friends at their Park Avenue maisonette for a postsummer catch-up cocktail party. As I navigated my way through the gilt, chintz, and tufted ottomans, I saw that their advisor was happily back on the scene, choreographing the tuxedoed waitstaff and mingling with the guests.

I air-kissed the wife. "I see he's back," I said. "You must be happy."

"Yes, I realized it was all a misunderstanding."

"Misunderstanding?" I asked.

"Oh, yes," she said. In her clipped European accent, she explained that she and her husband had worked out a new arrangement with the art advisor. "He charges a premium for his advisory services at auction. So we just created a new deal: a flat thirteen-point-seventy-five percent fee on everything including what we ask him to look at," she said. "You know, clarity and communication are everything. After all, I wouldn't want money to stand in the way of friendship."

Friend is a flimsy moniker in New York. It might apply to someone one meets at a cocktail party and two lunches later is a "great friend" based on grand commonalities like the private school admissions process or renovation dramas.

Then there are the friends for hire, the innately personable service providers who are sought out to fulfill social obligations, provide companionship, and offer courtlike flattery masquerading as friendship to those who can afford it. Heartache, though, sometimes occurs when relationship demands and financial arrangements are at odds.

"There is a market, a currency for paid friends in New York," Eternally Youthful Fashion Designer revealed over pecan-crusted seitan at Candle 79. "Some people need the money, and some people need the friends. It happened just last week."

"What happened?" I asked, eyeing her tantalizing vegan cheese platter.

"My staff was taking measurements, and my client's entire posse came to the atelier—you know, the hairdresser, the publicist, the stylist, the personal assistant. The housekeeper also came with sliced apples and almonds in a plastic bag as a snack. The trainer was giving my seasoned seamstress an opinion on the length of the garment. 'Make it shorter, make it longer. It's too tight.' Mostly though, everyone was, 'You look gorgeous.' You know, with the dramatic hand signal going to the mouth, like in an Italian operetta."

"That must have been aggravating," I offered.

"It's part of the business; if someone needs constant companionship and compliments, paid friends are ideal," she said, sipping her organic cola. "Honestly, it's just another form of addiction. I do believe that some care, but for the most part, someone's always on the make."

Over the next few months, I broached the topic of paid friends with a broad swath of people, and it turned out to be more taboo than sex. While the subject evoked knowing guffaws from some, others froze in their tracks, acting like I had stumbled upon a clandestine affair. (Guilty, obviously.) Others shrugged it off as something that clearly existed but not in their own backyard. No one I spoke to was willing to cop to possessing or being a paid friend. (Having a dominatrix seemed more acceptable.)

But one evening, I found myself at a dinner party seated next to the glamorous ex-wife of one of New York's most enigmatic commodities traders, noted for his custom suits and contraband supply of Cubans. Having received a lucrative divorce settlement, she was more than willing to open up about her ex-husband's assortment of paid friends. In fact, after I artfully plied her with Avión and an orange twist, she couldn't seem to talk about anything else.

"Everyone, and I mean everyone, was on the payroll." She played with her chestnut-size South Sea pearls. "When we first started dating, I was annoyed that so many people were always around. But I learned that powerful men all have posses."

"Why?" I asked.

"I think many really successful men don't actually have time for real friends. Their old friends are either resentful or bitter or ask for money, and the new friends are often competitive. In my opinion, very rich men have paid friends as an expensive filter, because they can control them. They love to manipulate everyone."

"Was that difficult?"

"It was actually more boring than anything, but I did see an ugly side to it—the laughing too hard at the bad jokes, the constant flattery, the jockeying for position, the tennis pro throwing the game."

"Did he view them as real friends?" I asked.

"The way he spoke to them was quite abusive actually, especially the good-looking ones. And they all took it."

"Did you keep up with any of them after the divorce?"

"Please! They couldn't wait to see me go," she said, toying with her endive and walnut salad. "The division of assets was a lot more complicated than the division of friends."

"How so?"

"There were a lot of assets and virtually no real friends. The people who pay get to keep the paid friends. No one was going to side with me when he was picking up the check," she said, nibbling on a singular endive, then pushing the plate away as if she had consumed an entire plate of lasagna.

"I am so full!" she exclaimed. "Look, let's be real. If he didn't have any money, he'd be sitting all alone in his apartment with a container of Häagen-Dazs and a bottle of vodka."

Sometimes, just being fun to be around is a currency that translates into social invitations, as it has for a bicoastal producer I know.

Sitting in the afternoon sun on the terrace of the Downtown outpost of Sant Ambroeus, a few glasses of prosecco clearly provided the proper amount of social lubrication to get him talking.

"In Hollywood, you're either in the starring role or in the supporting cast. I always said I was a paid extra." He laughed, his stylish frames glinting in the sun.

"Did you know any paid friends in LA?"

"Know any? My partner and I always joke we're America's houseguests. We're always being invited to fun, fabulous places, and it's always a seaplane, a private jet, five-star villas. Wheels up, baby!"

"Any downside?" I asked.

"Well, you're always on someone else's schedule—sort of like being a pet monkey. But when you're single and a free agent, you can enjoy the paid friend lifestyle at the drop of a hat."

"Do you see a difference in New York versus LA paid friends?" I asked.

"It's much more faux democratic in LA. There, the stars go out with their stylists in sweatpants for a latte. It's more formal in New York. The driver stays in the car; they're not having lunch with you at Da Silvano. In LA, domestic help really runs the house and raises the kids, because the actors and the producers can be away for months at a time. So they really are an extended part of the family."

"And in New York?"

"New York is more formal and diversified. In LA, proximity, traffic, carmageddon actually keep your group smaller. You don't just drop in on people; it's scheduled, and you tend to socialize only with the people you work with."

"How do the stars go about finding their paid friends?"

"LA is big on poaching. Once I started working with [one of the great female stars], everyone assumes if you're good enough for her, you must be good, so they try and poach you. And in LA, it's accepted that all the paid friends are waiting for their *All About Eve* moment."

"Such as?"

"I once went to a small dinner party with [the star] at [another huge star's home], and, of course, the personal chef comes out and wants to know if you eat meat or are vegan. At the same time, during dinner—it was an open kitchen—she's grilling pineapples and pitching a movie idea to my boss. Of course, no one blinks an eye."

"So why did you stop being a paid friend?"

"We're living here now, and we have our own lives to lead. Look, being a paid friend is complicated. When you're in the presidential suite, it's amazing; sometimes it can be emasculating, but I put my ego away a long time ago. Truthfully, there's also something reassuring about it."

"Reassuring?" I said, not believing my ears.

"Well, think about it. You have these incredibly successful and wealthy people who are at the top of their game and should be so happy."

"And?"

"And if they were so incredibly happy and satisfied, why would they need me to go to Hawaii to entertain them?"

While the perks, five-star holidays, and constant socializing all seemed somewhat fun, I started to hear more drawbacks to paid friendships.

"There's nothing more painful than a paid friend breakup," said a respected entrepreneur with an extensive infrastructure of PFs.

"How so?" I asked, looking out his office window across Manhattan to New Jersey, where life suddenly seemed much less complicated.

"In some ways, it can be frightening. You allow people access to your home, your kitchen fridge, your children's schedules. So let's say someone you've allowed 'in' falls off the wagon, shows signs of having a drug or alcohol problem." He leaned back in his leather chair fifty stories up. "You have to be careful."

"Careful?"

"If you have that nagging fear, sometimes, and I've done this, you actually have to pay them to leave. You have to, because it becomes emotional, financial, and reputational for the paid friends."

"Have you ever let a paid friend back after you fired them?"

"There was a situation where my wife's personal shopper started stalking her at events and stopping by with new items. I had to get firm with her."

"How did she take it?"

"Not well." He puffed on his cigar. "No one's happy when they're on the gravy train and the gravy train stops running."

Last Friday, I was being fitted for a cerulean velvet sports jacket at Jay Kos on Mott Street when an ominous black SUV pulled up outside the discreet storefront.

An old client from the agency business emerged and rang the buzzer, his trainer in tow. After a pleasant greeting, he immediately requested the same blazer (in a larger size, thankfully). His trainer, who was still in his yoga gear, pulled a few items for my acquaintance as well.

"Try these on—they'll look good on you," he suggested, yawning simultaneously.

"Do you always travel with an entourage?" I asked my former client.

"Why do you ask?" he said, looking at me squarely. "Are you writing a new story? I liked the last one, but my wife was offended."

"Wait till she reads the next one. It's on paid friends."

"Paid friends?"

"As in people who are friends with their decorators, trainers, stylists."

"Oh, I get it. She has plenty," he said, somewhat amused. "Why don't you ask him?" he then asked, pointing to his flexible friend. "He's a paid friend."

"No, I'm not. I'm your friend," the yogi said, somewhat offended.

"But you get paid."

"Yeah, but . . ."

"So you're a paid friend," he said matter-of-factly.

"I'd rather not," the yogi sniffed.

"I don't mind having paid friends," the client said, trying on a python jacket. "My wife is paid, and she's not even a friend. Just joking. You know me. I've had a few tussles in my day. Once you've had paid friends who don't argue with you, it's actually quite hard to go back to real friends." He laughed.

"That looks great," the yoga instructor said, eyeing my former client in snakeskin.

"You think I should buy it?" the client asked.

"Definitely. And you can throw this on the bill for me." The trainer picked a perforated cashmere scarf and wrapped it around his neck, Euro style.

"By the way, Richard, right?" The trainer stared me down.

"Yes?" I turned.

"That jacket looks awesome on you," he said, reaching into his pocket and extracting his business card with a photo of himself in a tree pose.

"Call me for yoga," he said. "You look like a rock star!"

"A rock star, huh?" I said, taking his card and tucking it into my wallet for safekeeping. "Tell me, anyone in particular?"

11. THE CUSTOMER IS ALWAYS WRONG

Welcome to the New Chef-Waiter World Order

I WAS RAISED TO BELIEVE the adage "the customer is always right," and as I've learned in advertising, it works better if one actually likes being in a service business.

I always thought this ethos would apply to the restaurant business, where serving patrons with a smile (even a disingenuous one) is part of the job description. However, lately I've detected an insidious strain of inhospitable service crossing over into actual hostility.

When an Upper East Side restaurant first opened its designer doors, I was thrilled to have a new eatery in the area, as the mom-and-pop places have all been replaced by glossy international luxury brands.

We joined friends who had booked a table in the dramatically lit main dining room. After air kisses and polite conversation, I asked for my chicken well done, since the newest fashion is to undercook everything as many of today's chefs think something "well done" is bourgeois and/or infantile.

I happen to like it that way and have resorted to begging the waiter to "burn it," just to get something fully cooked at the very least. (One trick is to ask them to butterfly everything for a greater probability of having the meat see the fire.) I sometimes use the line "apologies to the chef" to butter them up and also to let them know I'm not a fool.

But when the entrée arrived and I cut into the chicken, I immediately recoiled at the glistening, coral pink flesh inside. I called the waiter over. "I ordered the chicken extra well done and the inside is barely cooked," I said.

He rolled his eyes. "I'll take it back and see *if* chef will cook it more."

I motioned for my companions to eat as I waited for the final verdict. The server finally sauntered over as everyone else was finishing their meals.

"I'm sorry," he said flatly, bringing back my undercooked chicken, "but this is the way the chef prepares it."

"Excuse me?" I said as he placed the raw-ish carcass back in front of me. "You're telling me the chef will not cook my chicken more? It's almost *alive*." I was horrified.

"I'm sorry but that's the way the chef prepares the chicken," he said in a provocative gesture that was meant to say, *We are not interested in making you happy and there is a line of people waiting for your table.*

"That just happened to me here last week," said my friend, a powerful CEO of a public company, shrugging as I sat there, not quite knowing what to make of the situation.

"So why did you make the reservation again?" I asked.

"Janice (not his wife's real name) likes the ambiance. She loves the décor."

I lifted my wineglass and said, "Welcome, everyone, to the newest restaurant in town: *Chez Fuck U*."

There is and has always been a segment of the luxury market that borders on sadism. Perhaps there is an underlying philosophy that the worse you treat someone, the more they will want it.

This has spilled over to restaurants that overbook and do not honor timely reservations, keeping groups of people (including the elderly) standing and waiting for hours, while any random celebrity is whisked to a table. Waiters are now given license from imperious chefs to dictate to us how the chefs *want us to eat*, as if we are children who need to be educated on their ingenious and innovative preparation. And testy maître d's often affect a disinterested and unhelpful persona, their ennui on full display.

One day my dear friend the Impossibly Blond and Glamorous Socialite (TIBGS) and I were seated in the grillroom of a private club I belong to in Manhattan, where Mark Twain once frolicked. I enjoy the club even more as it offers elegant dining in a landmark mansion, its ambiance and gracious service uncompromised by surly staff.

TIBGS concurred that elsewhere restaurant abuse was getting out of hand. "The attitude and airs in this town are ridiculous," she shared. "And the behavior is topped only by the insecure patrons who put up with it."

"I agree," I said, watching the genteel waiter hand-toss the Caesar salad on a vintage trolley.

"I love the restaurants that make up prices," TIBGS offered.

"That's a good one," I said. "The best is the [well-known eatery] where no matter what you order the bill is always one hundred and fifty dollars a person. It always adds up to the same number for two people, whether you have no appetizer or two main dishes," I revealed.

She mentioned a restaurant once favored by all the social swans. "It was a home away from home for me," she recalled, "but if my friend [the famous proprietor] didn't like you, the place could be empty for all he cared. He would say there was no room, regardless of whether your eyes told you otherwise."

She continued. "The other day I saw a woman at an outside table at [major Euro establishment] feeding her Havanese off a plate with a spoon," TIBGS said in a tone indicating she was at once amused and appalled. "The restaurant said nothing even though everyone was outraged, because she is friends with the owner and happens to be titled."

"Maybe her new title should be *Her Royal Heinous*," I suggested, tasting the fabulous well-done club chicken. "At least the dog had good manners."

I recently joined some friends for a birthday celebration at an ultrahip Montauk restaurant. I would have preferred the old-school red-sauce Italian we sometimes frequent, oh so happy for the blue cheese dressing on the mixed green salad in the wooden bowls and the comforting eggplant parm and garlic bread. Once again, I bowed to my friends who prefer the "in" spot.

As I was sipping a refreshing watermelon vodka, my friend and neighbor appeared flushed. "They won't expand the table even though I told them it was my birthday," she said. It had originally been a group of ten—I detest group dinners but try to be flexible—and three extra friends showed up. While most normal restaurants would have just squeezed in three chairs or pulled the adjacent table over, the brittle maître d' who clearly graduated with honors from Chez Fuck U told my friend that the extra three people would have to sit at a table across the room, even though there was an empty four-top right next to our table of ten.

"Let's go." I happily stood. "There's a great old-school Italian I love nearby. They are so nice and accommodating and have the best red sauce in town. I am sure we can just pull up a few extra chairs."

"No," the woman said. "I like it here."

"What's to like? They won't even seat your friends near each other," I tried to reason, selfishly trying to push my agenda as visions of saucy meatballs danced in my head.

"We'll just take the table of ten, and they can sit separately," she said. "Let's just stay."

"Fine. I'll sit at the children's table," I happily volunteered, hoping not to have another group dinner.

"Oh no. You're part of the main group. We'll make the so-and-sos sit there since they joined last minute," she said. "Can you believe this treatment?"

"So why don't we all leave?" I asked.

"I really want to eat here. I love the view, and my friend said they have the best kale in town."

My dreams of hearty spaghetti with garlic bread were dashed by the cruel inevitability of rude service and trendy greens.

"I knew it was my fall from grace when they sat me in Siberia," said my LA-based friend, a well-known movie studio exec, of a high-profile NYC restaurant where they promptly gave him an inferior table after he had left his last high-profile post.

"What, were they reading the trades?" I asked.

He shook his head. "For years I'd been eating there and getting one of the prime tables, and then when I lose my position they give me a table so far in the back I was almost near the service entrance."

"How far back is far back?" I pried.

"So far back you've never ever even seen where they put me. The thing was," he said on the speakerphone from his car on the freeway, "that not that many people really knew about my departure. But THEY apparently did. Like they had a hotline to insider Hollywood gossip."

"What did you do?"

"I said to myself, 'I really don't like it back here in steerage, I better get another great job and quick.' Honestly, I had a great package and was considering taking some time off—but that was one of the things that threw me over the edge," he revealed.

"Have you been back since?"

"I stayed away for a time, but when I got the even better position, I decided to go back. Now I have a new strategy."

"What's that?"

"Now, every time I go there or to a new restaurant, I bring a celebrity with me."

On another occasion, we had just returned from Europe and were catching up with friends at a hip restaurant in Sag Harbor.

It took forty-five minutes of waiting and being jostled while they cleared and set the table. Finally they seated eight of the ten people in our party and everyone was famished.

"Why don't we order appetizers?" I offered.

"I'm sorry," the waitress barked. "We cannot take the order until everyone has arrived."

"Do you think it would be possible to get some bread and water?"

"I'll see what I can do," she said with the warmth of a prison matron.

"This is ridiculous," my friend Second Wife said as she waited for her houseguests to arrive, nervously looking at her watch.

"Why don't we up and leave and go to the pizzeria in town? They make awesome pizza and the best espresso," I offered.

Another guest at the table raised an eyebrow. "I'm not eating at a pizzeria. We just have to put up with the abuse. After all, it's August in the Hamptons. Where do you think you are? Capri?"

"I have an idea," I said to Second Wife. "Can you call Harry and Mark and see what their ETA is? If they are more than ten minutes away, you can put in their order."

The waitress returned to slam down a bread basket. "When are your friends getting here?" she said, rolling her eyes. "This can't be an all-afternoon event."

"I know." We now tried the honey versus the vinegar approach. "They apologize for their late spin class but my friend here called them and we actually have their order."

She tried to process something outside the norm. "Well, we can't take orders unless the whole party is here, but I guess it might work. But NO ORDER CHANGES when they get here." She pulled out her pad as she laid down the law.

"We promise. You're a dear and a delight."

"Doesn't everyone just want to leave?" I asked when she left. "This isn't exactly relaxing."

"Richard, there's nothing relaxing about the Hamptons in August. At least you had the opportunity to escape and go to Capri," my friend lectured me.

I raised my glass of white wine and toasted. "Welcome to Chez Fuck U."

No one has more restaurant stories than a Hamptons neighbor who is known for his *very specific culinary desires*.

"So there we were at [hot restaurant by hot restaurateur] when I asked the waiter if they had any salt and pepper. A reasonable request, no?" he said.

"I would think so," I said, eating my well-done egg white scramble at a diner that could be one of the few places on the UES that takes real requests seriously.

"So as I was saying, the actor/waiter came over and said, 'I'm sorry but the chef prefers that you do not eat his chicken with salt or pepper.'

"So I told him that if he was a good actor, his role that night was that of a waiter—and he should act like one and bring me what I want."

"And did he bring it?"

"It was a Mexican standoff. I eventually won it, of course, but I never went back. That said, it's a popular restaurant and it's packed all the time."

"That's the problem," I said. "Everyone is whipped."

The invitation was vague enough to make it interesting, and Dana and I decided to attend the Ralph Lauren event during Fashion Week in Central Park. We arrived close to the nine p.m. call time at the entrance to Central Park and Seventy-Second Street. As we exited our car, we were met by a group of helpful security and polite handlers who directed us to individual golf carts that drove us into the park and deposited us with the other guests. Ralph's staff, beautifully turned out in crisp summer white Polo shirts, were extremely polite, groomed, and beautiful.

"My, you look lovely this evening," a young man complimented Dana as we walked by.

"Would you care for popcorn for the show?" another graciously offered.

"Would either of you like water?" The chiseled waiter offered bottles of signature-branded Polo water.

We all gathered by the lake to watch the projected fashion show, the images creating a ghostly yet artful runway against the Central Park West skyline. After an image of Ralph took a bow to great applause, we were ushered out where a cart and retinue of Ralph Lauren waiters smiled brightly and offered the guests whimsical and creative Ralph's coffee cups to go. The way in which one of America's greatest success stories and luxury brands treated his guests in contrast to the appalling behavior now being served in many of today's supposedly best restaurants only reinforced why some people rise to great heights and others flame out.

If Mr. Lauren ever opens a restaurant in New York, I'd like the first reservation. I know the ambiance would be extraordinary and the service gracious and well turned out.

Finally, I'd be able to get chicken the way I want it. Now, wouldn't that be a fashion statement?

IV.

LIFESTYLES OF THE RICH AND INFAMOUS

12. WHY THE ITALIANS HAVE STYLE ALL SEWED UP

Fellow Americans, Don't Sweat the Sweater

BEING AN ADMAN, I always look at things in terms of slogans.

As an example, New Yorkers have responded to our new tagline for the New York Knicks: "New York Made." It is now available on the Jumbotron, T-shirts, and big foam fingers.

On a recent trip to Barcelona, having not visited in many years, I was reintroduced to the graceful, whimsical architecture and the vibrancy of the fabled port city, not to mention the savory chicken paella. That said, while I had found the citizens of Madrid business-like and elegantly turned out, Barcelona was the *least* dressed and stylish European capital I had encountered in recent years.

Everywhere I looked, T-shirts, fanny packs, and open-toed sandals abounded, despite the fact that there seemed to be more retail stores than restaurants. In fact, I was hard-pressed to see *one* well-dressed person despite checking into the regal Majestic, which houses the European luxury brands Loro Piana and Chanel.

One evening, Dana and I, our daughter, and her best friend ventured down to the chaos of Las Rambla to our favorite restaurant, the classic Los Caracoles, where Dalí was known to have enjoyed the roasted chicken on a spit and the intensely rich flan.

"What do you think of Barcelona, Daddy?" my daughter asked.

I turned to the group and declared, "If I had to pen a slogan for Barcelona, it would have to be 'Barcelona. Just rolled out of bed' or . . . 'Barcelona. Gaudi inspires, everyone else perspires.'"

Some might say that Barcelona is a city for the young, that the millennials are too busy partying to care about how they look. I might have fallen into that trap had Naples and Capri not appeared next on my itinerary. Indeed, I found it amazing just how young the Italian boys start when it comes to their fashion journey. As opposed to the fratlike style pervasive in Barcelona, in Capri the exact opposite occurs. Friday and Saturday nights the local teens from Napoli arrive off the hydrofoil and congregate in the town square, the teen boys parading in their perfectly ironed and starched collared shirts, Gucci or LV belts, and stylish shoes. Many already sport their initials on their shirts. I must confess it took me years as an adult to acquire the discreet *RK* initials that are emblazoned on my shirt directly under my rib cage. I found it somewhat humorous when I saw the Neapolitan teenagers doing it at such a young age.

"In Italy, clothes are a class statement," the Minor Contessa filled me in over her long espresso in the bar at Sant Ambroeus, her chunky gold link bracelet creating a bit of noise and drama on the marble counter.

"American men are, how you say, *solid*," she said in a disapproving way. "Very square." She blocked out a torso. "They all look like they are going to play golf in Minnesota when they get dressed. You know, polyester. A bit, how you say, *middle class*."

"Don't you think that's a bit unfair?" I asked.

"Richard," she said, stressing the *CHARD*, "in Italy, a suit is"— she used her hands like she was conducting an opera—"more than a suit; it's a way of life, who you are. It *places* you."

"Places you?"

"Yes. How is the fabric? Do you have hand stitching, workable buttons? Not everyone can afford it. In Italy it's as if a secret language. Take your suit. Napoli, yes?"

"Yes," I said, somewhat astonished. "How can you tell?"

"In my opinion, they only make suits like this in Napoli. The Milanese would argue, but that would be like saying the mozzarella is better in Milano than in Napoli, which we all know is a *fantasia.* And I can say that because I am Italian."

"And what differentiates it?"

"It's all in the shoulders and the cut of the lapels and pockets on the angle." She surveyed me critically. "My ex-husband had these suits. I am telling you it's a secret language. It says I can afford a suit for three thousand euros and I have the style to do it."

"Do you think it's particularly Italian?"

"Of course. I don't particularly *like* Italian men, and I can say that, being Italian, but, yes, they look good. My French lovers, and I have had a few, their suits are all very narrow and a bit serious, austere. They all wear the Hermès tie, not to mention the hygiene." She rolled her eyes. "I can say that because my grandmother is French and I'm Italian."

"And what do you think about the women?"

"I hate to generalize, but I think Italian men are better looking than the women and that French women, overall, have better style."

"And you can say that . . ."

"Because I'm Italian," she said, frowning at an American ordering cappuccino in the afternoon. "When I was much younger, I once had to lecture an American girlfriend. She had come to Italy for the first time and couldn't make the distinction between the men and the clothes and ended up dating a *waiter.*" She went on in a shocked tone, "The men are all handsome, dress well, and look like, how you say, John Travolta in *Sunday Night Fever.*"

"You mean Saturday night."

"Whatever night, *bello.*"

"So how did you save her?" I asked, anticipating a display of the Contessa's wit.

"I said, 'Susie, if you want to meet someone of quality, who has some money from a good family . . .' "

"Yes?" I said, hanging on her every word.

"Look at the shoes."

A whole generation of Italian women tried to look like Sophia Loren. As a teenager, when I first landed in Marina Piccola decades ago, I would first see all the Sophia look-alikes lined up in the port waiting for the open air taxis (the taxis in Capri are the only ones in the world that have striped awnings in candy colors): perfectly sculpted hair, gorgeous cheekbones, the impressive décolletage, small dogs. The rich ones flashed Bulgari bracelets and large emeralds (always the emeralds) and the middle-class women would sport the lesser-priced Pucci-style knockoffs (often in housecoats). They always looked impeccable though, no matter the resources, although the women who worked in the shops sometimes wore cheaper pleather sandals, which broke the illusion.

These days, the younger generation apes Donatella Versace: ironed blond hair, pillow lips and tanned skin, cell phones. It's alluring for sure, but after all these years I have to admit, I do miss the Sophias.

I have also come to the conclusion that it's not the women who make the statement these days, but the Italian men. Part Casanova, part soccer star, they are *peacocky* in a way that is unusual for the male species. Often their bodies are tall, lean, and lanky and act as the perfect hanger for their custom suits and designer belts. And they take their clothes very, very seriously. In fact, in Italy they actually have a word for the *art* of tailoring: *sartoria*, which clearly comes from having or conveying sartorial splendor.

On the Continent, I am impressed, for the most part, by the style of Italian men, and French women who radiate inner confidence. The English, in my opinion, by contrast, have a no-nonsense approach to their suits and outerwear. There is a durability to their tweeds and a masculinity to their Wellies and raincoats that subtly declares, "I am more interested in function than style—*so take that!*"

I was catching up with a Hamptons neighbor for a late breakfast at the Madison Avenue diner we frequent.

"When do you leave for Italy?" I asked over the egg white scramble, no butter, no toast, no potatoes ($10.95).

"On Sunday. I cannot wait." He applied butter liberally to his scooped-out bagel ($11.75) and identified a crispy piece of well-done bacon. "I have to get home and pack but I end up buying most of my things there anyway. You know, they have the best men's clothing in Italy."

"I know. Somehow, it just doesn't look or feel the same here." I thoroughly agreed.

"Look," he said, asking for more hot water, "there is one thing you have to accept; no matter what you buy, and how hard you try to dress that way—one just can't fully pull it off the way *they* do." He picked up another bacon slice. "You understand that because you have been going there so long," he whispered. "And, that at the end of the day, it's all about *the sweater*."

"*The sweater!!!!!* Of course." I nodded knowingly. When one is a twenty- or thirty-year vacation veteran of Capri, one understands *the sweater*. For those who may not know, every well-dressed Italian male of a certain age sports a carefully draped, colored cashmere sweater as he makes his way across the piazza for the *passeggiata* (the stroll). And it is draped ever so casually over the shoulders; with the importance of a film director and the insouciance of a movie star or politico. In many ways, it's the male version of the jeweled Capri sandal.

"*Well*, it goes without saying," I said. "They just know how to do it. After all these years, I just can't seem to get it right."

"Me either," he said. "It's maddening."

"No matter how many times I try, I just can't seem to wrap it the right way. They all find a way to look like Fellini," I offered.

"And it never, ever falls off on them," he said. "Do they glue it or staple it? Mine falls off all the time."

"It's the Italian version of the French cigarette that is essentially attached to the lip while they speak, and doesn't fall off. I am not sure how they do that, either."

"Correct. I have never, ever seen an American man able to either pull off *the sweater* or *the French lip cigarette*."

"Do you think it's a conspiracy?" We huddled.

"I just think it's another European act of superiority."

"I couldn't agree more."

"And they just seem to know when to pull out *the sweater*. Every time I try to do it, it's too hot. You know, I could be wearing a linen shirt from Capri, like the rest of them, but then a chill comes and they have all thought it out in advance. They just know when to pull out *the sweater*. Every time I try and attempt it, there's a heat wave and I look foolish. The Italians look at each other and smirk: 'There's another American trying to pull off *the sweater*.'"

"Mine falls off so much the waiters always fold it and put it on the back of the chair or sadly give it to me when it falls on the floor."

"That's the worst. The waiters always act so condescending. What they're really saying is we should not try and pull off *the sweater*."

"I have gotten to the point where I just carry mine. Dana thinks the way I drape it makes me look short," I admitted. Then I asked, "How many colors do you have yours in?"

"I would say twenty-five? And you?"

"The same. I do love seeing them all folded together. It makes me happy, my collection."

"Me too." He ate the last bit of his bagel. "There's nothing better than a good cashmere sweater. If only I could wear it like the Italians."

The white sangria with sliced peaches and lemons starts at 11:00 a.m. in Capri. Lazy days under the umbrella at Fontelina Beach Club are *molto rilassante*, very relaxing. I was under the umbrella, starting my exercise routine—a glass of the sangria and a swim—when an old friend, a native of Como, made his way over to say hello. I offered him a glass as we caught up. His family, one of the oldest in Italy, has one of the finest mills, and he oozed Italian chic with his movie star sunglasses and linen shirt and espadrilles.

"Yes, I think Italian style is defined by the '50s fantasy. It comes from that decade when we had the iconic leading men and women, when we had movies that traveled internationally as a point of reference."

"So you all have *La Dolce Vita* on the brain?"

"I think so. We start early. When you're born. Then you have your Communion at eight years old. You go for your suit. And of course it has to be the BEST."

"So it's a serious business."

"Of course," he said in a musical tone. "We have two thousand years on you guys. You know it's national pride; when you have the Colosseum and the Sistine Chapel, it comes from a genetic place of personal identity."

"Tell me about *the sweater*." I plied him with more sangria.

"Ah, the cashmere sweater," he said knowingly. "Well, now it might be a bit old school, a bit bourgeois. You know it all starts with the Italian mama. She wants you to take the sweater. 'Don't leave the house without a sweater . . . you might catch a cold from all the American air-conditioning!!!' Now maybe a bit cliché but you know we still have the sweater not to catch cold."

"And what do you think of American style?" I said as I applied sunscreen to my white skin, his tan skin oblivious to the rays.

"Well, I am an Italian who sometimes tries to dress American. I like the Steve McQueen, Jimmy Dean look. Maybe I shouldn't try to do that, and just dress like my fellow paesanos."

"And I shouldn't try *the sweater*."

"Yes, but you have more air-conditioning. Look, we're all obsessed by the other. I had an uncle and one day when I was growing up he came in with this shiny black shirt and I asked him where he got it."

"And?"

"And, he had been to America once and said proudly that he bought it in *Cincinnati*. He just liked the sound of it and thought it was cool. *Cincinnati*. Like it was Monaco!" he said in the most musical tone.

"I think they're living off their laurels," the reed-thin, English socialite said as we were dining on salmon wrapped in filo dough at the delightfully under-the-radar Periyali, back in New York. "I think Italian men had good style in the '50s, but they're living off fumes," she declared. "Italian men are cheesy. It's all about the lines 'I love you. I love you. *Belissima* . . .' They can't help themselves. They're wired for more than one woman," Tatiana (not her real name) determined. And I believed her, as she is a man-magnet for successful actors, musicians, and the occasional boy toy. Say what you want about Tatiana, she is known for her fabulous figure and incredible style. It's hard to argue with an innate fashion plate.

"Who do you think has the best style . . . the French?"

"I actually think the best style in Europe goes to London. The men are not overly curated. Anyway, it's more important to be fit than to be well dressed." She yawned.

"Perhaps you're biased because you're English."

"*No*, dahling," she said, fingering a toasted slice of pita. "I call it like I see it. I love America, but the men are the worst dressed on the planet. They have zero style and let their *wives* dress them. It's so sad. I do love your style, though. You're more European than American. And you have wonderful suits. Napoli?"

"How did you know?" I nearly choked on the pita.

"It's the cut. Very Neapolitan."

"What's the difference between an English suit and this suit, in your opinion?"

"In England, the suits are more conservative. They have a way of fitting by giving the *illusion* of being ill fitting, but the fit is, well . . . very English."

"And the women?"

"My friends all look good. Very little makeup. Right off the country estate and right into the Range Rover."

"And the best female style award goes to . . . ?"

"Why Sophia Loren, of course, dahling. Who else *could it possibly be*?"

The next day, I met my close friend, a very talented menswear designer, for lunch at the Downtown outpost of Cipriani on West Broadway to catch up on our summer vacations. Cips was exactly what I needed as I tried to ease back to my New York diet after two weeks of gorging on Southern Caprese cuisine. And when one is feasting day in and day out, one cannot just go cold turkey. Like one eases off cigarettes or heroin, there has to be a methadone version of Italian food withdrawal to help the body recover. My friend, who is a Paleo, wasn't indulging. However, I always love getting his POV, as he doesn't have opinions as much as free-floating declarations!

"I just think Italians wear it better," he stated clearly.

"I agree." I viewed the glistening *melanzane alla parmigiana* lasciviously. "But how so?"

"The fit of the clothing is closer to the body, and they are more casual about it than the Americans. When American men get dressed up, they look *constipated*," he said, not caring that I was eating.

"The Italians are also in better shape," he continued. "They're fit. Americans are afraid to sit down because they don't want to wrinkle their suits."

"So you aren't a fan of American style?"

"They look like assholes."

"So who is buying your clothes? You live in America." I tried to shoot holes in his theory.

"I design for myself."

"Meaning?"

"Meaning my customers—they're all rich. They're all in shape. International. They're not wearing velour sweatsuits in Vail. That's not Italian style."

"What do you think of *the sweater*?"

"Italians wear the sweater because it's cold, Americans wear it because they saw an Italian wearing it in a magazine but then it's one hundred and twenty degrees."

"What do you think of the French?"

"I think French women are the best. Chic and a bit messy. French men have good suits but for some reason they wear those long shoes and look like elves. The tips are always five inches past their toes. I still think the Italians do it better. That's why I manufacture my suits in Italy. They only want the best of everything. The best fabrics and tailoring. They may not have a lot but it's always the best. It's the opposite in New York."

"That's pretty harsh."

"It's the truth. In the US we hate our jobs because we need to make money. In Europe they take being the best seriously. The best tailor, the best waiter. They're happy every day doing whatever they are doing. It's the olives. Even the man who is making espresso at the gas station, so there's a pride and therefore the style and clothes are the best quality. We're all working so hard that we're miserable. But that's the reason we work so hard: to make money, be miserable, and then fly over there for great style and a great bowl of pasta. For five days of happiness."

Two days ago, I decided to duck into Via Quadronno for a double espresso as I had a little too much fun the night before. As I stirred the espresso with the diminutive spoon, an attractive older and aristocratic woman walked up to the bar. I did a double take as I noticed she was a *Sophia,* the mocha velvety skin, the high bust, the coiffed hair—all cheekbones with the Sophia spectacles and dripping in Buccellati. She looked me over from head to toe.

"*Scusi,*" she said. "*Che ora è?*"

"I'm sorry, but I only speak menu?"

"Menu? I don't understand."

"I have been going to Italy for over twenty-five years, but I only speak menu."

"Now, I understand." She laughed. "I'm so sorry, but I thought you were Italian, the way you were wearing your sweater."

"Don't be sorry," I said with a smile. "You actually just made my day." I smiled at my Sophia. I stood up straighter, the lavender cashmere sweater falling ever so effortlessly over my shoulders, perfectly in place.

13. LET THEM EAT KALE

Extreme Dieters Ruining Dinner Parties for Everyone Else

"HOW CAN ANYONE THROW a dinner party today?"

A noted hostess bewailed the current state of culinary affairs in the drawing room of her regal Park Avenue duplex, in one of the grandest of grand co-op buildings. It was ever so expansive yet artfully understated, with parquet de Versailles floors dutifully waxed into the kind of dull patina old money truly understands.

We were having late-afternoon cocktails as the sun dimmed through the sheers, and she waxed poetically about the dire straits of entertaining today's power couples versus the glorious dinner parties of yore.

"Let's say you have six couples for an intimate dinner," she said. "Nowadays, this one has a nut or shellfish allergy. This one is now a vegan. The wife is a vegetarian but eats cheese. The other couple eats no dairy. The new thing I hear is this Paleo craze, where people want to eat like a caveman. Someone's assistant even called my chef to inquire as to whether it was sockeye or farm-raised salmon." She harrumphed. "Can you imagine? It's gotten to the point where I should just put out a stack of take-out menus."

"So what do you serve?" I ask.

"I once tried tofu, but women don't like it because of the estrogen. Julio (not the chef's real name) does a roasted, Italian-style vegetable dish drizzled with balsamico and olive oil. People *adore* that."

I took in the creamy yellow walls, perfectly adorned with Scalamandre silks and satins in shades of egg yolk and freshly whipped French butter. "What would you like to serve if you could?"

"If I had my way, I would do what [legendary socialite known for her stick-thin figure] used to do in the '80s," she said. "I would just serve designer meat loaf and mashed potatoes. Everyone just loved it."

"So why not now?"

"I tried it once, and no one touched a thing except for [a former leading politician] who had two portions. Sadly, those days are long over." She sighed. "No more crusty French bread, seafood soufflés, lamb chops with mint jelly, or filet mignon with a dollop of butter."

I asked her if she thought people were missing out.

"Of course I do. No one's glowing or juicy anymore. Just take a look though at their skin," she whispered. "They're all *sandpaper*. They all look like prisoners on furlough—every last one of them."

The old adage "you can never be too rich or too thin" has had a renaissance on Madison and Park. Competitive and restrictive eating and exercise regimens have transformed power players into Power Rangers. Cross-training, spinning, boxing, yoga, and martial arts are the tools of the trade along with nuts, seeds, berries, and juices. Fat is considered a weakness.

"People I know are *vaporizing* right before my eyes," Second Wife whispered over a belated holiday meal at her home, twinkling above the UES skyline. I often refer to her as my *second* wife as she is one of Dana's and my closest friends, but thankfully, her husband gets the Amex bills, not me.

"I feel everyone's constantly at an ashram." She shrugged, taking a paper-thin slice of holiday turkey off the platter her chef prepared. "People are starting to look like bobbleheads."

"You're certainly known for your figure," I offered.

"Thank you," she said. "You know, I work at it, but it's getting to the point where it's no fun anymore."

"How so?"

"You also have to enjoy life. People describe others as obese if they are only twelve to fifteen pounds overweight. And it's not like everyone looks so good so thin. You start seeing the drawn, leathery skin. I call it 'pointy face.' They look ten years older."

"It *is* crazy. If a centimeter of fat hangs over the belt, your husband is filing for a divorce," I said, sadly. "How do you feel about that?"

"Not my *problemo.*" She shrugged again.

"That's because you're disciplined," I said, toasting her.

"The bread basket is *over,*" she declared. "Welcome to lollipop-head land."

According to a recent study, two-thirds of the US population is overweight or obese. But not in the 10021 zip code.

"It really is one of the great ironies that in the olden days fat people were rich and poor people were skinny," a leading nutritionist told me over seitan at Gobo. "The higher the income area, the lower the weight."

"Do you think it's also about fashion?"

"It's really about everything," she said, crunching on a piece of fresh lettuce. "By the way, veggies are a great replacement for bread when you're eating hummus. And two almonds in the morning quell hunger."

I nodded. "Do you think people are taking all this too far?"

"Everyone needs certain nutrients, but underweight is better than overweight in my opinion. And from what I know, they don't even make couture gowns over a certain size, so it pays to be thin if you're in that crowd."

"Where's that? Hollywood?"

"Yes, but certainly in New York."

"And where else?"

"Palm Beach for sure," she said. "Oh, another tip: boil asparagus until very soft, and use it in a blender as a base for low-cal guacamole."

"Thin is the new luxury," the *Über*svelte and Fit Real Estate Developer remarked on the terrace of his recently developed multimillion-dollar penthouse.

"In my father's day, there were the social x-rays. The women looked after their weight, but the men were large." He reeled off two '80s titans of nouvelle society, one a financier in New York and the other a legendary magnate in Beverly Hills. "They could eat prodigious amounts of food. Their girth was considered powerful.

"Today, the new successful men are careful about their weight and want to be thin. Old-school fat is considered slothful. Old school was prime rib; new school is parmesan-roasted kale."

"But what do you really crave now and then?" I asked.

"The roasted carrots from ABC Kitchen."

Certainly, I know Chef Dan's culinary skills. "He's the best," I agreed. "But don't you ever want a good, old-fashioned cheesecake?"

"No, do *you*?" he asked, as if I had suggested dropping bath salts at a rave.

"Actually"—I leaned in—"when I need a fix, I have seven-layer cake shipped in from the Five Towns."

"I wouldn't do that. Just like people used to frown on smoking, now they frown on bad eating," he advised, giving me the tour of the planted terrace replete with Palladian-style French doors that some lucky high flier would soon inhabit.

I marveled over the kitchen.

"Yes, it has everything . . . and even a wine cellar," he said, listing the latest top-of-the-line appliances and luxuries.

"For the dinner parties where no one eats anything," I joked.

"If they're smart," he said seriously.

"For successful men, do you think it's about competition as well?"

"Everyone wants you to know they're dieting, juicing, working out six days a week. It creates an image."

"Of?"

"Of don't fuck with me."

"Isn't that *darling*?" one of the grande dame socials remarked, peering at the cylindrical tuna tartare and avocado column topped with the waffle-fried potato chip.

"It may look wonderful, but be careful," another dinner partner commented. "Tuna is high in mercury."

It's going to be a long *evening,* I thought as the black-tie gala got under way. The packed evening at the Plaza underscored New York's robust charitable circuit, where much good was being done while much-photographed women were allowed to also break out their latest couture and big stones. After the customary speeches, a famous entertainer gave a miniconcert, making a fee but still getting accolades for doing a charity benefit.

"Is there a vegetarian plate?" I asked the white-gloved server as she tried to foist a Flintstone-size side of beef in front of me with a dauphin of Lyonnaise potatoes.

"Why, that's clever of you to ask. I have to think of that the next time," the grande dame added, her Plymouth Rock–size canary diamond coming dangerously close to shattering my wineglass.

"Are you vegetarian?" she inquired, her platinum, lacquered bouffant and ageless skin triumphing over any apparent lines. "It seems the trend these days."

"I'm a pescetarian," I explained, "who likes his vino." I motioned to the server for a country-club pour of white wine.

"Well, you can always do what I do," she said. "Eat a little snack beforehand. My late husband taught me that trick; a piece of low-fat string cheese saves the night. Look around. Hardly any of the women eat anything, because they don't want a poof in their gowns, and the men have all been ordered to stay away from red meat because of high cholesterol."

Around the room, people were either observing their main course or politely pushing the food groups around.

"It's such a waste of food, especially for a charity involved with the homeless and the *hungry*," she acknowledged. "But for fifteen thousand to fifty thousand dollars a table, you have to serve beef."

Later that month, Dana and I braved the elements to celebrate a friend's birthday party at a club downtown. We knew it would be a good party, as the social butterfly and her real estate magnate husband have vast quantities of fun, among other assets. It is rare to see a step-and-repeat at a birthday party, but there was Society Photographer, snapping away. I sidled up to the bar and ran into a music industry mogul, a former Hamptons neighbor.

"How have you been? You look great," I said, noticing his vastly diminished size, his head outsized to his hips.

"I lost eleven pounds—no wheat, no rice, no flour, nothing white. I was a size thirty-six jean in college, and now I am a thirty-one." (The new dieters, I had learned, often feel compelled to validate their dieting odyssey with stats.)

"What's been the upside and the downside to the new sleeker you?" I asked, sipping on a white wine.

"The upside is my girlfriend likes it. I feel better."

"And the downside?"

"No more Italian food. That's been the hardest, although my credit card bills are better since I stopped going to [well-known, overpriced Italian eatery]."

"Well, you're so disciplined. There must be something else going on?"

"Of course. It's competitive. It's all about control. You try and control every aspect of your life, and you want to be the best you can be."

"And better than everyone else?" I asked.

"How did you know?" he asked. We fist-bumped.

"I'm not as crazy as some of those Paleo dudes," he added.

Finding a Paleo wasn't hard. I just looked down at my own dinner party list and called to speak to a friend who, for more than two years, has done a total transformation, or "mansformation," as I prefer to call it. I met him after his cross-fit workout at one of the only *five* restaurants he would eat at in the entire city of New York. At a table at ABC Kitchen, he ordered split pea soup, and we had an honest conversation about the new rules of the *über*disciplined.

"So," I said, "you look even more buff since the last time I saw you."

"Superripped."

I got right down to business. "So now tell me what you do if you're invited to a wedding or bar mitzvah?"

"We always bring our own food," he said matter-of-factly.

I was fascinated. "You bring your own food to someone else's event?"

"We bring nuts and berries and pack a green juice. For dessert, one hundred percent cacao bar."

"Where do you put it?"

"In Marissa's (his wife, not her real name) purse," he said with the seriousness of a trial lawyer.

"She doesn't carry an evening bag?"

"At a dressy event when she cannot bring a larger bag—a mommy tote—we stop for dinner."

"And how do you eat if you bring the tote?"

"We dig into the bag when no one's looking. No one knows," he confided.

"Why don't you just order the vegetarian plate?"

"The vegetarian plate will undoubtedly be some bad kind of carb, rice, white potatoes, and pesticide-sprayed vegetables from a big-box retailer, or they try to pass off green beans or asparagus in faux butter from not grass-fed cows. No one in my family would eat that, not even the dog."

"Do your hosts ever get insulted?" I asked.

"I'm insulted," he fumed. "It's all processed butter, grain-fed beef, and farm-raised fish."

"Do people ever tell you you're too extreme?"

"All the time. They're just out of shape and jealous," he shot back.

"Do you think what you're doing is restrictive?"

"It's neither competitive nor restrictive," he said, flexing his superripped bicep in his wife-beater à la Jake LaMotta. "I look at eating as fuel. Eating is not social. It's a fuel event."

"So what do you do at a small dinner party?"

"We either decline, eat beforehand, or I bring my own food and cook it. I did that in Paris recently, at a very swanky party, I might add. I went right into the kitchen and made a giant vegetable omelet. Everyone was obsessed with it. The caterers were upset."

"Were you embarrassed?"

"I would never be embarrassed. I'm embarrassed for them and the way they eat."

"Clearly," I said, feeling ever so out of shape. I decided to have a piece of crusty roll with my soup, to his horror.

"Look, I sleep better now, exercise better, fuck better. My skin is better. I'm in the best shape of my life," he declared. "Oh, and I also wear a T-shirt that says, 'I hate vegans!' "

"What do you have against vegans?"

"Look at them. They don't have orgasms."

"Really?" I said.

"How can they?"

I was having a holiday lunch at Da Silvano with a friend who is an author and a well-known *New Yorker* cartoonist and just happens to be the proprietor's wife.

"No one eats bread anymore," she said, shooing away the bread basket.

"Do you think people still eat?"

"I think they do. They do when they come here," she said. "Why? Do you think I look fat?"

"This wasn't aimed at you. You look very thin actually," I said.

She looked visibly relieved.

"Do you think men are the new women when it comes to dieting?" I asked.

"This manorexic trend has to end," she said. "No woman wants a man who's skinnier than she is. Why? So he can make my ass look fat? I don't find that attractive at all. Please, no woman wants to see a man with camel toe."

"Well, certainly that's not something I have to worry about," I

said, taking a healthy-size forkful of the *melanzane alla parmigiana.*
"I like a proper lunch with wine, of course."

"That's why we'll always be best friends," she said. "Because
you love food, and so do I, and I feel thin around you." She peered at
me. "Although you have lost weight recently."

"Yes," I said. "It's been a battle."

"Wait, do I look fat?"

"No, you look thin," I said. "Do I look fat?"

"No, I just told you that you look thin, which made me think I
was fat."

"What does one thing have to do with the other?"

"Because no women wants to sit next to man who's thinner than
she is."

"Fine, tell Silvano to bring on the pasta with truffles."

Since so many people have replaced solid food with juice, it was only
natural to pay a visit to the founder of one of the hottest juiceterias in
the city, Juice Press.

"Vanity is a great impetus for change," he said, driving his BMW
along Sixth Avenue with the authority of a race car driver. "Whatever
your path, it leads to the highest road. I'm forty-five, but I'm buying
time like I'm twenty-five."

"Don't you ever miss the steak?" I asked.

"I'm long past the crave stage," he said, making a getaway-style
turn onto Sixth Avenue. "No, I don't eat inflammatory, processed
foods. I'm also less at risk for diabetes, stroke, etc. I have detoxed
myself to get that poison out of my system."

I took him in. "And you look pretty fierce with all those tattoos.
So no chocolate cake?"

"I had a European friend who also tried to get me to be more
balanced like him . . . but with *his* way, cigarettes and foie gras, he
couldn't walk up a flight of stairs. Balance to me is being fit and
exercising with twenty-five-year-olds."

"But don't you miss food?" I asked as he veered the car onto
Madison Avenue.

"I view juice *as* a meal, not a replacement of a meal. It is food unto itself. I keep myself very close to fruit and vegetables," he revealed.

"And what would you do if I invited you to a dinner party?"

"I don't get caught up in the shark feeding tank of a buffet. If it was a sit-down dinner, I would just have a salad or some fruit."

After visiting a juice bar full of private school girls ("They are always ahead of the curve"), Marcus drove me home with green juice. "You and your girlfriend must come for dinner," I offered. "I'll serve you juice in a Limoges bowl."

"I have a better idea," he offered. "Why not have a juice-a-cue, like a barbecue? We'll bring the machines in and start juicing."

Although I had been fairly certain the idea of competitive longevity and its attending regimens were an NYC phenomenon, the next day I flew to Las Vegas for the famed Consumer Electronics Show, where a client was launching LYVE, a personal media solution. With 150,000 visitors descending upon the city, I took refuge in the glamorous Wynn Hotel and Casino.

After a night flight, I had a late dinner at the marvelous Red 8. I discovered that every restaurant at Wynn has a vegan menu. Over the next two days, I sampled a breakfast of vegan blueberry pancakes and vegan sausage at Tableau and vegan chicken dumplings so realistic I would fly to Vegas just to have them.

While the vegan chicken dumplings were the most exciting thing to happen to me in Vegas, I do still have erotic dreams of a strip steak, in a strip club on the Strip.

That's why people cheat—on their diets.

14. FROZEN

The High Cost of High Maintenance

"I CAN'T IMAGINE HAVING a full-time job, children, and being able to get it all done," the Auburn Heiress declared as we stood in line at a buffet dinner hosted by one of New York's most beneficent financial geniuses. Not everyone in finance knows how to entertain these days, but at Chez Hedge Fund, the wine is always flowing, top drawer and Petrus, and it's never the usual suspects or entrées.

"Well, you look *marvelous*," I said, surveying her Chanel-clad physique, suddenly realizing I may have overdone the pronunciation and sounded like a bad imitation of Ricardo Montalbán. "How much time and money does it take to look this good?" I asked, realizing her looks appeared frozen in time since I first met her, having nothing to do with the nineteen-degree weather outside.

"I would say twenty to thirty hours a week," she said, playing with the stack of pavé Love bracelets. "As for the cost? Whatever it costs. Anyone who tells you anything different is lying."

"Do you even have time to see your friends?"

"Oh, I see them at all the appointments."

"As in?"

"Well, let's see," she said, spooning the avocado, ruby grapefruit, and fennel salad onto her plate. "After spin class, I get my coffee, and then I go to Valery [Joseph] for my blowout. Then I might have a dermatologist appointment for Botox, a filler, a laser, or a peel. I think derms are the new plastic surgeons, although I'm not against a snip snip when duty calls. Ça va! Then it's time for lunch, you know, somewhere casual like Fred's or Sant Ambroeus. Then I'll make a few important calls."

"And then?"

"Well, you know, the mani-pedi, waxing, acupuncture, lasering, not to mention the ultimate appointment."

"Ultimate?"

"Yes, the eyebrow lady. Booking an appointment with her is like getting an audience with the pope. One has to maintain or suffer the consequences," she whispered in an ominous tone.

"Which are?"

"We all know what they are, Richard. Why dwell on the negative?" she said, her clipped tone expressing a slight *froideur* before drifting off, leaving a trail of Jo Malone's orange blossom in her wake.

"It's either a kiss or a curse," one of New York's most successful women offered over a recent lunch at the Lambs Club. "Maintenance is like an addiction. The more you do, the better you look, the better you feel. If you don't do it, well . . ." She paused with a dramatic flair that suggested a butter-cookie-and-pound-cake-fueled descent into slothdom.

"You can say that because you're as skinny as a sixteen-year-old and look twenty-five," I said, admiring her Studio 54–worthy vintage DVF wrap dress.

"Thanks, darling. Although I have found there is a real cost; the skinnier you are, the better you look, the meaner some of the girls are to you," she said over perfectly grilled Brussels sprouts. "They want nothing to do with you if you're a size two or less. But I always say, 'Be high maintenance but maintain yourself.'"

"That's because you're so smart about everything you do," I said, referencing her imprint on New York's fashion landscape.

"Let's get one thing straight about *smart*," she said, smiling innocently. "No man looks at a woman and says, 'I want to go to bed with her because she looks smart.' "

"Hair is the biggest expense: six days a week," the Social Powerhouse declared at an eight-course dinner she was cohosting at Le Bernardin.

"Six days a week is quite a commitment. Must cost a bundle," I said, tasting exquisite Dover sole while being hip-checked by a cool blonde in sable and diamonds who was table lingering, having an in-depth conversation about lip threading.

"Actually, getting my hair blown daily saves time and money," the Powerhouse declared to a few carefully groomed nodding heads.

"How so?" I inquired.

"Well, they do a better job than me, and the more you do, the bigger the discount. I also get to make dinner reservations and catch up on texting."

As I looked around at the immaculately turned-out group, no one was without a professional-level blowout.

They clearly shared the self-maintenance ethos of our Social Powerhouse, reputedly one of the bigger spenders and high fliers in NYC. "My husband's grandmother always said, 'Women should be like well-manicured lawns: don't wait until the weeds pop up,' " she said.

"Grandma was a very sage woman," I agreed. "She wasn't European, was she?"

"No. A well-manicured New York lawn. European women are meadows and wildflowers."

Having spoken to a series of Uptown girls, I knew it was serendipity when my assistant, Carol, told me I was having lunch later that week with a soigné British socialite at EN Japanese Brasserie on Hudson Street.

"It's totally not a myth," she said over tasty black cod and hijiki salad. "I mean, just *look* at this hair. Do you think I *ever* have it blown?" She gave her bedhead-style hair a finger comb. "It's sexy *not* to have blowouts."

She turned to see the famous and iconic Japanese wife of a member of one of the greatest bands in history enter the restaurant dressed entirely in black in a severe suit, sunglasses, and a jaunty chapeau. My black cod tasted all the more authentic because of her presence.

"I don't ever want to look like a generic American," she said, sipping her Sancerre. "Less maintenance is more."

"I think you're incredibly chic and original, but you don't do hair, makeup, maintenance?"

"I'm not that woman. I don't want to look perfect. I just use French oils and go to the gym for a run or get a manicure. It's all too sanitized here. In Europe, natural confidence is sexy."

"And your friends—do they do nothing and feel the same way?"

"My girls, the ladies so-and-so, just wash their hair, put on their Wellies, and off they go in their Range Rovers."

"So they're not blow-drying for their lordships?"

She leaned in. "Do you know what the European secret is?"

"No. Do tell," I said, leaning over my bento box.

"I only spend on beautiful, sexy, and elegant underwear!"

"Don't they have that here?"

"No. It's all colored, cheap, vulgar, and tacky. American girls wear the worst underwear. I see it at the gym. I'm talking about showing up at a man's apartment in trench coat, heels . . ."

"And?" I gulped.

"And underneath is a divine corset, garters, stockings. Ding dong, he'll never get over it," she said, looking over at the former *Rolling Stone* cover story.

To complete my very own maintenance program, early that Friday morning I made the pilgrimage (a few doors down) to see my dermatologist for my quarterly skin check, which I advise all to do.

After I stripped down to my skivvies, the doctor, an eternally youthful and ageless practitioner to socialites and stars, had this to say.

"One can look good at any age," she said. "You just have to know when to stop. I really think my patients look good and young. They take their maintenance seriously. We can do so much today."

"Is there ever a time when you advise cutting the skin?"

"Of course," she said. "There comes a time when it's time for that, and then we recommend plastic surgeons. But there is a cost to doing too much."

"What do you think is over the line?"

"When people come in with magnifying mirrors. They'll point out a line or look at themselves in direct sunlight with a magnifier. That's a bit much. No one looks at someone else they meet through a magnifying lens."

It was yet another Alaskan evening as we once again made our way through the frozen tundra, with Dana wrapped in a J. Mendel white powder puff.

At a dear friend's birthday celebration, at which half-naked models were posed as Greek sculptures, all the toasts to the birthday girl included references to her looking exactly like her daughter.

On the dance floor, I once again ran into the Social Powerhouse, this time turned out in a form-hugging Hervé Léger (that revealed not an ounce of body fat nor a hint of panty line) and studded Louboutins.

"How is your article coming?" she asked. "On my favorite subject, maintenance?"

"Fabulous. Look around," I said. "It's perfect. One can't tell the parents from the children."

"That's why my friends and I love your pieces—they're all so true!"

"Well, let me ask you," I said, as we danced to "I Will Survive." "Did you learn all your beauty and maintenance secrets from your mother or do you have a sister?"

"Not at all."

"How do they look?"

"Terrible. They're both overweight and dumpy with wrinkles."

"Do they like clothes?"

"No," she said, laughing. "They wear black leggings and nurses' shoes. They do nothing."

"What do the men in their lives think?"

"There aren't any."

"Do you think there's a correlation?"

"Anyone who I ever met who said they don't do anything and that 'a man should love me for me' was single," she said dryly. "I just wish they maintained or I could help them. They really should be dating."

"Can I get you a drink at the bar?" I offered.

"I'll have a margarita, no salt," she said.

"Frozen or regular?"

"Frozen," she said, dancing off with a group of private school girls who looked so similar I couldn't tell who was who.

15. THEY'RE SHAVING A BUNDLE

Uptown Manscapers Struggle to Keep Up with the Ladies

AS I AM AN ADMAN, a Monday morning in April found me in a TV recording session in the heart of Williamsburg for my client the New York Knicks. Once we turned onto Bedford Avenue, every adult male resembled a cross between Abraham Lincoln and Man Mountain Dean: beards, tattoos, checkered flannel shirts, and a distinct lack of grooming. Equally interesting were the array of creative hairdos from ponytails to topknots. While I thought the Brooklyn grooming aesthetic was distinct, it only seemed odder after a dinner I had later that week.

I am not usually a fan of group dinners, but by the time Dana and I arrived at the Mark, there was a boisterous and fun group of people I call the twenty-carat crowd ("One carat for each year I've had to put up with him"). The assorted group took their seats at the round table, catching up on spring break itineraries, while depleting the wine cellar and bar in one fell swoop.

"He looked ten years younger on the beach," the Social Powerhouse declared as her husband suddenly exposed his tanned and now hairless chest for all to see.

"You should do it too, Richard," he pleaded, as he discussed his waxing and laser treatments. (This was not the first time someone tried to recruit me into hairlessness.)

"It's really not an issue for me." I shrugged. "I have lots of hair, but it's all on my head."

"You're lucky," said my close friend I jokingly refer to as Second Wife. "There's nothing *worse* than back hair."

"Gross," said another wife at the table, plucking an olive from her husband's martini. "Men have to take care of themselves or face the consequences."

"You'd rather be with a younger guy?" I asked.

"Absolutely not," she said, twirling her gold, man-size Rolex. "If he kicked the bucket"—she pointed to the poor guy—"I'd rather go with a girl."

Several of the women nodded in agreement.

"That's what happened to [an Uptown girl]. She just took off with [a molten successful businesswoman]."

"She's so *hot*." A few of the women nodded, seemingly impressed.

Two days later, I was walking down West Broadway after a lunch of black cod and miso at Nobu when I ran into two members of a well-regarded financial family.

I air-kissed the sisters in the street.

"We loved your column on parents who take drugs. It's so true," one sister declared.

"What's your next piece on?" the second sister asked.

"I'm trying to decide if I think there is a story about women who prefer women and how their husbands are now waxing and lasering to keep up with their wives' desires. Are Uptown men turning into the new lesbians?"

"Yes, I was just going to say your next piece should be about girl-on-girl," said the second. "It's such a trend."

Sister Number One nodded in agreement. "The husbands are all into it," she said.

"Why's that?" I started taking notes in the street on my iPhone.

"Because it's not a threat, and it's a turn-on," Number One continued.

Two added, "All these women are making out at social events, and the husbands stand around and watch."

"Do you think men are waxing to keep up?" I asked.

"Definitely," she confirmed. "If your wife were interested in a landing strip, either you buy one . . ."

"Or get one," Number One added.

When my assistant, Carol, and I went over the week's schedule, I was pleased to see that she had arranged a breakfast at the [exclusive private club that doesn't like press mentions] with an old client who I'd kept up with, post the account and his divorce. He just so happens to be one of New York's most conservative fellows (think Andrew Carnegie) and at face level I have no business being friends with him. He had been at a white-shoe banking firm I used to handle, and I always assumed he slept in a bow tie or an ascot.

The years have been kind, I thought as we sat down to a breakfast.

"Of course I shave my privates," he stated matter-of-factly as I choked on my watermelon slice.

"*You* actually manscape?" I said, realizing I had hit the jackpot.

"Ever since the divorce, I shave, and I must tell you, the feeling is quite *piquant*, a bit sensitive and tingly," he said.

"I'm sorry, but I would never have assumed," I said, wide-eyed. "A bit TMI but *sooo* interesting. You shave? You don't wax?"

"I will never wax again with a part that's movable."

"Why do you manscape?" I asked.

"You know," he said, "the younger ones like it. After the divorce, I went out with many women, and the ones I liked all requested shaving or waxing."

"And?"

"Well, you're in the advertising business. You need to give the consumers what they want. If you were on the market, you'd be marketing it in different packaging, I can assure you. And the grooming does make one appear, well, more virile," he offered.

"How's your sausage?" I asked, changing the subject.

The next week, I met a famous '70s party girl who maintains her style-icon status for breakfast at the Crosby Street Hotel, where she ordered grilled figs with honey and nuts and retrieved a bagful of vitamins while rummaging around in her bag, exposing an aromatic bag of weed. The dark sunglasses, bedhead hair, and African jewelry were all amiss, suggesting she was still recovering from a night at Studio 54.

"No one had a landing strip back then, in the '70s," she said with a yawn. "Everyone had big bushes. The men had 'fros and hairy chests and wore poly bellbottoms. It was *sooo* sexy."

"Do you think it has changed?"

"Back then, we did it for sport. Everyone did. The wrap dress came on and came off."

I was intrigued. "What do you think of all these men waxing and grooming?" I asked.

"I'm informed by a different era." She looked at me in the sunlight. "The idea of a man who has no body hair is actually repulsive to me. Your industry ruined it for everyone, darling. The million-foot-high billboards with all these adolescents with six-packs look like Leni Riefenstahl propaganda."

"What about women?"

"What about them?"

"Do you see women with women as a trend?"

"This is your problem. You're in the advertising business, and everyone wants to be *defined*, a *brand*; everything is a *trend*. Let's be clear: I've been with women off and on my whole life. I think women are *sooo* damn boring. Give me a man any day—either a young one who wants some experience or an old one," she said, fingering a bag of weed from her YSL purse as if she wanted to roll one right then and there but knew it was still too early.

As the breakfast came to a close, a young, buff woman approached the style icon. She introduced us.

"This is Alicia (not her real name)," the icon said. "She's my trainer."

"Where's your studio?"

"I live in Williamsburg, but I do privates in the city," Alicia said. I asked her about the preponderance of beards in her neighborhood.

"I don't go out with any of those guys," she said instantly. "They don't like me, and I don't like them."

"Why not?"

"I'm too strong for them. I think they're all feminine trying to act masculine. And they like girls who look like them. Tall, skinny, with tattoos and partially shaved heads. Not my thing.

"Plus," she continued, "they all go to these barbershops. It takes hours to get those beards looking like Mumford and Sons."

The following weekend, the sun broke through, offering up the promise of walks around the reservoir without a winter coat and the possibility of alfresco dining. Dana and I decided to pay our old friend Hassan a visit at Orsay and roll the dice for an outside table on the terrace.

"Hi, ladies. What will you be having today for lunch?" The waiter approached us from the back. He reddened when he realized I was a man.

"Oh, I'm so sorry. I thought, well, it's just from the back you have long hair, and I thought you were a woman."

"No worries. It happens a lot," I said, shrugging and laughing it off as I ordered my salmon burger and *frites.*

After taking the order and departing for the kitchen, I turned to Dana.

"Do you think my hair is too long?"

"Don't you dare," she said. "You keep your Bon Jovi locks for as long as you have them. Although if I want to start a rumor, all I have to do is kiss you from behind."

"It's not too much?" I asked, suddenly feeling insecure.

"Do you know what men would give to have your hair and be mistaken for a woman?" she asked innocently.

Clearly, they're spending real money trying.

V.

THE RICH ARE IN-DIFFERENT

16. SOCIAL CLIMB-OVERS

The Ultimate Workout

IT WAS AN UNSEASONABLY WARM October Thursday and despite the heat, the Fifth Avenue outpost of Harry Cipriani was filled with more *ciao*s and *bonjour*s than one could possibly count. Dapper Sergio showed my guest and me to my regular table, and it didn't take Greenwich Banker and I more than two Bellinis to realize we might have been the only two English-speaking patrons *en vue*. When did Fifth and Park Avenues turn into the Via Montenapoleone or the Avenue Montaigne? Why was New York now filled with so many fleeing Europeans? *Was it wartime or just economic wartime in the Eurozone?* I asked myself.

I wondered, that is, until a familiar figure barreled his way through the crowd in his slick custom suit and anachronistic Brilliantine slicking his hair, making a beeline to yours truly.

"Richard, so good to see you. It's been *ages*." He oozed saccharine flattery.

Not long enough! I thought to myself as I smiled politely and felt both obligated and somewhat put out to introduce him to my lunch companion—which I knew was one of the reasons he descended on me so quickly. Peter Poseur (not his real name) was always one to

sniff out a new acquaintance when he saw a glint of a peeking Patek
or thought there was a hint of social *possibility in the air*. He had a
sort of social radar that was uncanny.

"Listen," he said, adjusting his orange silk cravat, "Sage (his
second wife, not her real name) and I are hosting a dinner party at
[awful trendy restaurant where I know he is not paying for his meals,
but has a deal with management to bring in guests] and we would
looove to have you and Dana come." He surveyed my friend's suit
to determine if the sleeves had workable buttons, therefore ensuring
Greenwich Banker was worthy of poaching. Confirming his answer,
he immediately went in for the kill and issued my guest an invitation
as well.

"We're having it for our *dearest friends*, the so-and-sos (a
magazine-worthy couple).You will just *adore* them, I can assure you.
They're just *marvelous*." He beamed at the association. "I won't *hear*
of you not coming. Who knows, you might get a new account out of
it for that new agency of yours." He smiled, the points of his teeth
comically looking like fake Halloween wax fangs. "In fact, I'll put
in a good word for you," he offered like an oncoming bullet train of
tactless superlatives.

"Are you OK?" he said suddenly, noticing my profound silence.
"You look a bit pale."

"Is the Heimlich maneuver in order?" My friend surveyed me.

"I'm fine. It's just I already know them," I said, rolling my eyes
(which I should not have done).

"You do?" he said, crestfallen.

"Yes, Peter," I said, plucking a breadstick and indicating my
desire to end the conversation. "If you recall, I introduced them to
you. You called me and asked me to make the introduction when you
were on the committee of that charity event."

"Oh," he stuttered blankly, "that's right." He paused. "Well, I
hope you can come anyway," he said, slinking away into a sea of
*arrivederci*s.

"I hate when that happens," Greenwich Banker sympathized.

"It's fine," I said. "You just witnessed one of New York's greatest
workouts." I shrugged.

"Workouts?" He looked confused.

"Yes, like spinning or boxing. I call it friend jumping or the *social climb-over.*"

"You mean like social climbing?"

"No, climb *over*. When someone climbs *over* you to get to a friend or a business associate. It also has nothing to do with a comb-over, but it's equally unattractive."

One can read the annals of Plato or Plutarch and come across ancient reports of social climbers, as human nature hasn't changed much in thousands of years. That said, since the recent financial crisis, there seems to be a level of naked ambition that continues to have a shock-and-awe effect on people of reasonable manners. While many gossip about the climbers, fewer give any attention to those climbed *over*, those who have been left behind and have to deal with hurt feelings and the emotional wreckage of feeling and being *used*.

"My friend actually knew her when she first arrived in New York." Our Lady of the East River sniffed, and I knew the story would come tumbling out. Remember that Our Lady, my friend's blue-blood aunt, is one of the guardians of Old New York Society. I happen to be a fellow board member with Our Lady and we have become unlikely friends.

"I met her *years ago*, when she was married to her first husband. Poor young man. He married her against his mother's wishes, given that she was a"—she lowered her voice and punctuated the word in a scandalous tone—"*nanny*. Not that there's any *shame* in it, but no mother—especially a European—in my circle wants her son to marry the help."

"Was she a beauty?" I asked, thinking of TV shows I had grown up with like *Upstairs Downstairs* or the current *Downton Abbey*.

"Healthy in that blond sort of way that young men find attractive. Glowing cheeks, right off the farm in the Midwest. *No* social background to speak of." She raised an eyebrow.

"Doesn't sound out of the ordinary." I lifted my Limoges teacup of Earl Grey as she declined the tapenade on the peppered cracker from the liveried servant.

"It wouldn't have been . . . if she stayed with him. It was a standard-issue Pygmalion story: the manners, the clothes, the family name. In less than a year she was another person. He launched her but isn't given the credit."

"I have to hand it to her. She had *ambition*."

"She certainly did."

"And what happened to her?"

"Well, you know who she is." Our Lady mentioned a name I indeed had heard of. In fact, I knew her socially.

"I had no idea it was *her*." I shook my head as I marveled at her self-creation.

"Of course, she was still a *newlywed,* but she climbed right over her first husband to marry the richest financier she could. And sealed the deal with children and an immense stock portfolio." She shook her head.

"I daresay she is one *very* smart woman." I nodded.

"And now affects that she comes from a well-to-do family that has lineage." Our Lady paused. Then she went on, "Well, it would have all worked out perfectly, given her social climb-over, as you say."

"Yes." I knew the story intimately.

"Except that the second husband fell in love and she discovered the tryst. It's a story as old as time," Our Lady explained.

"Although I like her, I think it's just deserts," I said, offering Our Lady the dessert plate. "Tart tatin?"

"Flattery will get you everywhere," F. F. Grace declared. (F. F. Grace as in "fall from grace" . . . Not his real name but he knows I use that as his nickname since he was a victim of an insider trading scandal, leaving him penniless after having lived in enormous wealth for a few decades.) We were breakfasting at the Crosby Hotel, feasting on sublime grilled figs and a plate of carefully arranged orange segments, dried cranberries, and a drizzle of honey.

"When I had boatloads of money, people were tripping over themselves to get to me. Now, of course, only old friends like yourself who really care for me want to see me."

"That must be difficult," I acknowledged.

"Actually, it isn't. It's been very free-ing. When you're *in* the game, the game takes over. When you leave it, you start over with a new game and new rules."

He explained his social theory over the beautiful jasmine flower expanding effortlessly in the glass teapot.

"Now that you mention it, I did see the social climb-over, and I understood it was all part of the game. Even though I didn't really want to acknowledge it at the time," he said.

"How so?"

"The type of people who climb over their friends when they want something are playing the game. Most, though, do have good person-alities and charisma. That's why they're good at it. If they lived in France during the reign of Louis XIV, they would have been court-iers. They know how to flatter, how to maneuver. They make you feel good about yourself, always laughing at your jokes, always inter-ested in what you have to say. They key in on you and make you feel important and special."

"And?"

"They manipulate the circumstances so they can create their *own* crowd out of their friends' friends and keep the introducers at arm's length. They are smart enough, though, to charm and flatter the old friends, to stay on their good side so they keep being invited to their parties to keep meeting new people. When it comes to protocol, they know that when they are going to entertain the new acquaintance, they should also invite the couple who introduced them in the first place. Instead, they roll the dice and try to distance the new acquain-tance—let's say that's you—from their old friends. They erase the introduction because it complicates their plan to invade your life. And the next thing you know, they're right into *your* inner circle. Before you know it, you walk into your pantry and they're helping themselves to your stock of 1942, or uncorking the Petrus in your kitchen, like it was their own."

"They maneuver everyone out of the way." I nodded knowingly.

"Yes. And go in for the kill."

"Stash and I are climb-over victims many times over," Billionaire Mistress declared over dinner at Via Quadronno. "One of the most difficult ones involved a very close couple we were friendly with, with whom we no longer speak," she said, her stack of pavé diamond Love bracelets jangling.

The conversation proved as delicious as the delicately fried sole and aerated, whipped mashed potatoes.

"What happened?" I pried shamelessly.

"We introduced our long-term friends to another couple at one of our dinner parties, and they requested a dinner for six. We obliged, trustingly, as we actually enjoy introducing friends to friends."

"When did the alleged climb-over occur?" I took notes like a police officer on the scene of a crime.

"To make a long, drawn-out story palatable: our friends became enamored NOT with the other couple, but with the other couple's ultra-rich *parents*."

"Wow, that's a climb-over story extraordinaire. What happened?"

"My *real* friend called me on the phone clearly upset, saying he went to his parents' house in the Hamptons and *this couple and their children were staying there for the weekend.*"

"Wow, that's crazy. They're not your average climb-overs. They're mountain climb-overs."

"I was mortified. I had no idea that these so-called friends would turn out to be *leapfroggers*." She sniffed, still smarting from the scandal.

"How did you and Ken (not her husband's real name) handle it?"

"After weeks of anger and disappointment, on our end at least, they begged us to meet them at the hotel bar of the Peninsula since hotel bars are businesslike and fairly anonymous."

"Exactly," I concurred. "Did you tell them you were mortified?"

"Of course. They tried to explain that they had met the couple's parents at a family dinner and had become friendly; they said how charismatic they were. But let's be honest . . . why would a couple in their thirties be hanging out with people in their seventies unless they wanted to mooch the summer house or an investment in their business?" She shook her head and ate a sliver of garlic toast.

"We shall never know, but only can surmise." I nodded my head in agreement.

"I do relish what we said to them, though," Billionaire Mistress shared. "I said, 'To make an introduction to dear friends and have you become friends was our intent. But to hear that you are hanging out with our daughter's best friend's *grandparents* is more than odd—it's inappropriate. You embarrassed us socially.'"

"Have you ever seen them again?" I inquired.

"She tried to approach me when I was having my hair done at Valery Joseph, but I just waved her away. No one climbs over me and gets away with it."

"And what happened to them?" I asked.

"All I can say is they moved to the *West Side*."

Two weeks ago Dana and I decided to host a holiday at our home in the Hamptons. What was meant to be a small gathering of ten or twelve eventually turned into a guest list of fifty. Since it was meant to be a buffet and not a seated dinner, we were flexible and as Hemingway once said about Paris being a "moveable feast," I just accepted we were having "an expandable buffet." That said, days leading up to the holiday were filled with an inordinate amount of requests, cancellations, and rebookings.

A number of couples called with regrets and then when their logistics changed again, they called to ask if they could still come. Darla Van Heusen (my sister) asked to bring three houseguests of hers. My friend's wife's two sisters were in town, not to mention people showing up as tagalong guests the night of. Then, out of the blue, another invited couple brought along two notorious friend jumpers. At first I was taken aback, but then thought it might make for good material so let them come.

Since we have a mixed bag of friends, it was interesting to see people the night of the event socializing and meeting new people, some gravitating to the unexpected (i.e., charming and poor with boring and rich).

The day after the event, I received a number of e-mails and texts, most thanking us for the party with gracious accolades. One or two people sent e-mails asking for one of the guests' numbers. Then, as if on cue, Dana and I received an e-mail from the Notorious Friend Jumper, who oozed compliments about the evening (a bit too over-the-top since he was not officially invited) and suggested a dinner for six, indicating he and his wife enjoyed meeting a wealthy and prestigious couple whom we are close with.

"Do you want to do the dinner for six?" I asked Dana.

"Not particularly," she said.

"Why is that?"

"The only reason the so-and-sos are interested in the so-and-sos is for business."

"Yes, that's clear," I admitted.

"I see a friend-jumping situation happening before my very eyes," she said in an annoyed tone.

"Well, they did the right thing by inviting us," I said.

"The only reason so-and-so invited you," Dana said knowingly, "is because he knows *you* would pick up the check for dinner. And I've come to the conclusion that *we don't have to pay twice*."

And with that, she sent our regrets.

17. THE WEALFIE

Like a Selfie, but with More Money and Status

DANA AND I VENTURED DOWNTOWN to yet another trendy restaurant (that I am constantly being dragged to) with friends. As we waited for our table, the Aging Platinum Benefactress emerged from the crowd and made her way over for a double air kiss, leaving an imprint of her potent *eau de parfum* on my suit jacket.

I had always admired APB. She was impeccably turned out in vintage Chanel, and her earrings had the handiwork and markings of the artful Place Vendôme jeweler. She hadn't changed in years but looked somehow prettier and visibly softer. Had her work been performed by the Impossibly Blond and Glamorous Socialite's husband?

"How have you been?" I asked, as she withdrew her iPhone from her handbag.

"Here," she said, shoving under my nose a photo of her scantily clad daughter who was seductively posing at the infinity pool of the fabled hotel in Antibes. "Isn't she beautiful?"

She scrolled for more photos, then retrieved one of her son. "Isn't he *gorgeous*? I think you should use him in one of your campaigns."

When I hesitated to respond, she practically shoved the iPhone into my sight line. "Isn't he GORGEOUS???" she implored again, showing me photos of him in upscale action poses, playing polo and shooting clay pigeons. Her tone demanded an affirmative response.

"You must be very proud of him. A handsome young man," was all I could think of. "And I am sure he has all the social élan of his mother," I added, raising an eyebrow.

"He's the next big thing. I'll have his agent call you. I heard you have that new agency, SWAT something," she said. "Sounds *cute*."

It wasn't the first time I had been subjected to someone's "wealfies," a term I coined to describe selfies taken in a luxury context that confirm one has money, status, and social currency.

While poor digital manners have abounded for years with people attached to their devices during dinner parties, driving, and, yes, even at funerals, there is a new level of coarseness that one must contend with. While the selfie institutionalized digital narcissism, the *wealfie* is used as a weapon, a way to convey crass materialism and lord one's social standing over others.

Does anyone really care about someone else's children? Hear ye, hear ye, the answer is a resounding NO. Unless I have seen your offspring grow up and I actually like them, no photos, please. And I certainly don't want to see your teenage offspring in model pose being transported by Sherpas with name-brand luggage.

"I really don't know what to say." I turned to Dana after we were seated. "I would have thought that manners would have translated to technology but even APB is acting like a vulgarian."

Les gens de finance aren't exactly known for their witty or stimulating repartee, but there I was at a cocktail party in the impressive limestone *maison de capital-investissement*, trying not to bump into the conceptual art, which oddly seemed to be installed in the stately home's most highly trafficked areas. Why not just move the soup cans out of harm's way? *Sérieusement!*

Someone, who was consuming Avión tequila at an alarming rate, was leaning against a rare canvas of an abstract artist one only sees in museums when I was approached by the host. He introduced me to the imbibing Master of the Universe, George (not his real name) who was eager to make my acquaintance.

"Oh, you're the ad guy who writes those columns. My wife hates you. In fact, she told me if I ever run into you to tell you that you shouldn't be writing about us," he said matter-of-factly.

"Do I even know your wife?" I asked.

He mentioned the familiar name of an imperious woman I often see berating waiters in tony restaurants.

"You know her, right?"

"I was raised that if you don't have anything pleasant to say, don't say anything at all."

"I think we are going to be friends." He laughed. "I agree with you, by the way. I'm like one of your articles where they stay together because of the money."

To my host's credit, he picked up on my discomfort and tried to broker a change of subject.

"You should see George's new apartment on the hundred and fiftieth floor (not his real floor) of the newest building on Fifty-Seventh Street (not his real address)."

"Here," George said, taking out his iPad to show me what eighty-five million dollars buys. "Let me show you the view." The *ultimate* wealfie.

"It comes with this kitchen," he said. "But we're ripping the WHOLE THING OUT." He scrolled through half a dozen photos faster than you can say *nouveau riche*.

"I feel like we just had an intimate moment, and I just met you," I said coyly.

"How's that?"

"Well, are you going to show me a compromising photo of your wife or your balance sheet next?"

"I like you." He laughed. "I think we're going to be friends. Let's make dinner plans."

"Well, it will be hard to make dinner plans if your wife hates me."

"Don't be so sensitive. She hates me, too."

"Listen, it was nice meeting you and seeing your assets," I said, jumping over the metal floor sculpture in a dash to escape the situation.

"It's the new show-and-tell, with an emphasis on the *show*," the LA-based Power Agent said over dinner at Le Cirque. (Is there a better Dover sole and French fries in New York, I ask?)

"If you're sitting in the front row during Paris Fashion Week, you would absolutely take, as you say, a *wealfie*, and when you get back to New York you casually show it to your girlfriend and everyone knows where your seat was. It's digital bragging rights."

"Sounds like a lot of work." I was addicted to the fries and started searching for more before I caved and put in for a second order.

"It actually isn't. I see it in LA all the time. So-and-so is at a party and they take a wealfie next to a star at someone's dinner party and then it's shown discreetly to friends. A wealfie tells a million words about who they are and who their social circle is. I guess you can call it personal PR."

"I just find the whole thing incredibly annoying," I admitted.

"It's *supposed to be annoying*," he said. "They show you wealfies because they want the other person to feel less than."

"You know you could be a psychotherapist." I was impressed.

"I already am. But in LA we're called agents."

It has been my experience that divorced men either get remarried immediately to whoever will sleep with them or they go through what I call a *grazing* period. I was at a business meeting at the Downtown outpost of Cipriani with two other married gentlemen when a recently divorced businessman who joined us whipped out his iPad with the artichoke and avocado appetizer.

First came the wealfies of mansions, Bentleys, polo, and five-star resorts. Next, the model girlfriends.

"She's five-foot-eleven and Norwegian," he said, pulling up a lingerie shot. "I see her when I'm in LA." He shrugged as the married men salivated. "This is my New York squeeze." He pulled up a photo of a blond hyper-supermodel in a swimsuit.

"Is she real?" one of the men asked.

"I promise you it's all real. Every inch." He smirked, showing the table his conquests.

"Congratulations on all the fun you're having," I offered.

"Well, I do also want to meet someone, so if anyone knows anyone let me know."

"You just showed us four models. Isn't that enough?" I asked.

"Of course. But I also need someone I can have a conversation with. I don't speak supermodel," he said.

"I think this falls into the 'Uptown problem' category, Ned (not his real name). I don't think anyone is crying for you." I laughed.

"I know," he said, scrolling away. "I'll just have to suffer through it." He sighed.

I was extremely happily biding my time, alone, thank you very much, watching one of my children at a sporting event when a fellow parent (from another school) plopped himself down and started talking to me despite the fact that I was clearly ensconced in *Barron's*.

"How was your summer?" he asked.

"Interesting. I had a very un-Hamptons summer," I offered.

"The Emptons?" He laughed.

"So I see you read my columns."

"Yes, very funny."

"How was yours?" I asked, not really interested in the answer but trying to be polite.

"Here," he said, taking out his iPad. "We were in Greece. I rented this yacht." He showed me the 150-footer. "The best crew I ever had. Then we sailed to Istanbul. We stayed at the Four Seasons. Check out the view of the Bosporus from my suite. Then we flew to Venice. I had a craving for pasta." He showed me a photo of the bowl of penne.

Thankfully the whistle blew and I collected my child, said my good-byes, and called my lawyer from the car.

"Let's trademark the term wealfie," I said, then called someone who works for me to take out the URLs for wealfie.com and wealfie.net. "If I'm going to have to put up with this kind of behavior, I might as well own it."

18. THE REVERSE BRAG

How It Puts One Over the Top

IT WAS A STARRY, STARRY NIGHT at one of New York's most grand and storied hotels. Sleek, ominous town cars and darkened, menacing SUVs waited in a black line of auto dominoes, pulling up to the curb to deposit some of New York's most glamorous couples (likely and unlikely) as they emerged in front of the landmarked structure. Once inside, one heard the lowered voices and luxurious swoosh of the long chiffon gowns as they swept across the marble floor, and the subtle click of the heels of the Louboutins and Jimmy Choos, and of the cameras. Not the cold, hard glare of the paparazzi's flashes, but the discreet and knowing smiles of the society photographers and columnists who were making the rounds, greeting the guests as old friends. Dana and I had purposely missed the cocktail hour (too much socializing), and we made our way into the ballroom for dinner.

"Do you know who is performing tonight?" I turned to ask my dinner companion, the younger wife of an older Texas Oilman, once I was seated. I knew there was a trend of getting A-list talent to secure an event's status as A-list.

"I hear they got so-and-so." She mentioned the name of one of the world's most famous musical superstars, who was also an A-list actress.

"Wow," I said, nodding my head in approval. "She's one of the greatest."

As the star was introduced, she made her way out on the stage to a low-key smattering of applause—not exactly the ovations she is used to.

"Hi, y'all," she said sweetly into the microphone. When she heard the impolite conversation and lack of response, she became visibly agitated.

"Does anyone care that I'm here?" she asked, like an angry, wounded bird, wobbling a bit on her heels as she took in the slight.

"I just hope she doesn't go on and on and do a whole concert," my dinner companion said, rolling her eyes. "Three or four of her biggest hits and an encore would be perfect."

"She has so many hits, though," I said, a bit perplexed at her reaction.

"You know these *show people*," she declared. "They just go on and on and never know when to stop."

"Well, I for one am excited. I mean, it's a private concert from one of the world's greatest stars." I shrugged.

"I heard her at my friend's fiftieth. Been there, done that."

There was a time when people wanted you to know what they had acquired, or the premium experiences they had that you didn't or couldn't have. With the recent distribution of wealth, there has been a democratization of luxury goods and the attending experiences. Now housewives in New Jersey can carry the same bag you have and go on the same vacation you do. The trappings of status and luxury have diminished, causing a group of *über*wealthy to raise the table stakes for experiences and status in order to once again stand out. A-list stars are now de rigueur for weddings, charity events, bar mitzvahs, and sweet sixteens. Vast donations to private schools ensure one's children get extra privileges (i.e., extra test time and note takers in classes). Mansions have become private hotels, and art collections have given way to one's own private museum. While the newer nouveau riche use typical in-your-face tactics to convey their wealth and status, there is a trend among the truly rich and ultrasophisticated to use boredom as a new bragging tactic. The "whatever" attitude allows them to brag, but in a more subtle way that ensures no one can accuse them of outright bragging since they are feigning *humbleness*. I call this "the reverse brag." However, the reverse brag is a dangerous tactic as it renders the bragee extremely unlikable. That said, likability does not allow them to accomplish their nefarious braggadocio goals. And while perhaps not a new tactic, reverse bragging is one step above outright bragging as the bragee views it as a more sophisticated type of boasting that is meant to ape old money. For me, however, it only serves to further ostracize the person as a "sophisticated bragger"—worse than a new and clumsy one.

"One day I'd like to come back as my own children." Real Estate Mogul shook his head in what I knew would be a classic reverse-brag move.

"I mean, drivers, bottle service at sixteen, vacations in St. Barths on yachts. . . . I never had that growing up. I think I may have been too lenient and indulgent," he proclaimed, looking for acknowledgment and sympathy over the most divine hash browns and Dover sole meunière at Nicola's.

"You give in to them too much." His wife, Doreen, shook her perfectly coiffed head dramatically. "It's a fault of his. Larry (not his real name) just can't say *no*," she said in an admiring tone that affirmed to all he was a Big Spender!

"That's not true," he said, shooting her a glance. "When Brent (not their son's real name) wanted a Lamborghini for graduation, I did say no. I mean, who would buy their kid a Lamborghini for college graduation?" He threw his arms in the air like on a game show.

"I agree," I said. "I had a Subaru in college and thought I was styling."

"Larry, come on." Doreen gave a mock look of disdain. "Here's a man who says he won't buy his son a Lamborghini but then turns around and buys him a Porsche right under my nose. I mean *really*, Larry. He just can't say no," she insisted.

"Clearly, Larry has a 'no' problem," I said, now looking at the couple with entirely new eyes. Suddenly, I realize they are doing the reverse brag *together*, as a couple. I realize that this is part of the modus operandi. Whether intentional or not, they have a sort of prerehearsed routine akin to a finely honed vaudeville act.

"Well, a Porsche isn't exactly pâté, Larry," I noted, raising an eyebrow.

"No. I went out of my way to buy him a pre-owned Porsche. He has to understand the value of a dollar," Larry explained.

"And his four-thousand-dollar-a-week allowance?" The wife dramatically accused him of more largesse. "Really, Larry, you just don't know how to say no."

The waiter brought the bill and laid it down on the table with some delectable biscotti. "Let's split it," Larry said.

"My treat," I said.

"Sure. Thanks," he said, withdrawing his card.

"I thought Larry couldn't say no," Dana joked in a nonjoking fashion.

"I don't know what's worse, having to go to the Oscar or Cannes parties," the Famous Hollywood Film Producer complained when I ran into him at James Perse in the Malibu Mart. He looked relaxed, despite his schedule and the incessant juggling of statuesque and European blondes.

"What do you think, Famke (not her real name)?" he called out to the famous underwear model in tow as he emerged from the dressing room in surfer shorts.

"I zink you need a larger size," she replied, yawning.

"Maybe she's right." He patted his prodigious stomach. "It's that awful chef I have for the kids. I mean, it's just too much food and too formal. I'm not a formal type of guy. Just give me a salad and a burger, but the ex wants the kids to have filet mignon," he said in a classic reverse-bragging mode. "How's the ad biz?"

"It's been really interesting. Working on lots of great and interesting projects," I said.

"You know if didn't go into the movie biz, I would have loved to have gone into advertising. Really, LA is so tiresome, the parties, the cars, the women . . ." He motioned to Famke dramatically.

"Not to mention your homes?" I decided to help him reverse brag and see if he would take the bait.

"Don't you know it. I just want to sell the house in Beverly Park. I mean, who needs thirty thousand square feet. I need an apartment or maybe just a simple six thousand square footer."

"You're just a *simple* guy, Don (not his real name). That's what I have always loved about you."

"You see, you get it because you're from New York. Most people here are so stupid. It's the sun and all the working out and the implants. It just goes to the brain. That's why I want my kids to get out of this state. But I think they're too low-key to go to Princeton or Yale." He shrugged.

"I understand. Maybe they need to take a year off when they graduate," I suggested.

"Look, I was a f**k-off when I was their age. They have discipline and are smarter than their dad. But even though the Ivies would grab them up in a second—given their grades, scores, the athletics I've paid for—they just don't see the point in going to one just to say 'I go to an Ivy,'" he reverse bragged. "So they're going to Europe for the year traveling before they go to [think Ivy of the Ivies]."

"Maybe you should move to New York?" I said, goading him.

"I would in a minute. After the award season, which I hate, I'm going to look for a place. We'll have dinner."

"Great seeing you. Love the shorts."

"That's what I love about his stuff. Just California Casual."

As we were boarding Jet Blue (with the luxury of extra legroom) one weekend heading back from a shoot in the Caribbean, I ran into a noisy New York family of five I knew all getting on the same flight, nannies and strollers and all.

"Hi, Richard. So great to see you. Were you down here on vacation?" the father asked.

"No, I was on a shoot for a client."

"Sounds exciting."

"How about you? Vacation?" I asked.

"We were down for the weekend for a party."

"Fun?"

"The party was great, but I didn't love the villa." He mentioned an older resort on the island. "A bit run down."

"That's too bad."

"Everything was chipped and broken. The bathrooms were a disaster," the wife added, as she shook her head and moaned.

"I mean, not that we should be complaining," Stew (not his real name) said. "The so-and-sos (the hosts) paid for everything. It was for a fiftieth birthday. I wanted to upgrade, like I usually do, but I didn't think it would be in good taste."

"They really should send someone from that resort to see the villas on [the island where Stew and his wife own a home]. It's generous to put guests up, but a hovel isn't exactly a vacation." Mrs. Stew sniffed as she reached into her Bottega bag for Purell.

"But the party was fun?" I asked

"Really fun. They brought in so-and-so." (She mentioned the very same famous female A-list singer I had seen at the charity ball.)

"That must have been fabulous," I said as I placed my roll-on in the overhead compartment. "She was great at [annual mandatory charity event]!"

"I just wish she would have done two or three songs and then we could have danced to the DJ," the wife complained.

"I mean, how many private concerts can you go to?" Stew said.

"I think for your fiftieth I'll just get a DJ. Enough with these famous acts," the wife said.

" It gets tiresome after a while," Stew said. "And it was nice of [the host] to offer to fly us private, but I think it's important for the children to experience flying commercial," he reverse bragged.

"Yes," the wife said, yawning. "Once or twice."

When I got back to New York, I dropped off my luggage, showered and changed, and ran to a dinner at one of my all-time favorites, Shun Lee on the East Side. We were meeting our friends, the so-and-sos, and the well-attended service proved smooth sailing after a bumpy flight. As we caught up over lotus root and sole with ginger and scallions, discussing fun topics such as Ebola and the crisis in the Middle East, we strayed to somewhat lighter fare, timely divorces and breakups.

"Another one bites the dust," I said, citing a couple we thought seemed to have it all but were always fighting.

"Was either having an affair?" I probed.

"Not that I know of," my friend said, sipping his tequila. "I think New York can just be particularly hard on certain couples."

"I know what happened," Dana said, rolling her eyes.

"What?" the table asked.

"They just ran out of things to brag about," she conjectured.

"I buy that." I explained my theory on reverse bragging. "They clearly weren't meant to be. They were always contradicting each other in public. And you cannot reverse brag if you do that. Not possible. Think about it. There are couples who are so good at it they seem to have a prearranged press release." I mentioned another couple who artfully knew how to reverse brag together and have a long-term, seemingly solid marriage.

"So you don't think it was an affair—they just weren't on the same page?" My friend processed the idea.

"In order to execute the reverse brag, your partner must reverse brag with you, or at the very least not contradict you," I explained. "It's the golden rule. He who has the gold makes the rules."

"Take the so-and-sos," Dana said, stating her case. "They just celebrated their twentieth wedding anniversary. They're the couple that says they don't believe in having any help and she doesn't believe in nannies, but when you go over to their home they have ten people in shifts of two. Twenty years of solid reverse bragging. And she never shares her resources."

"And he always toasts her 'doing it all.' By herself," I recalled.

"You see? Now that's a couple." Dana laughed.

"Couples that reverse brag together . . . stay together," I said. "Honey, we'll have to start reverse bragging."

"About what?" Dana asked, wide-eyed.

"I can tell people that no one reads my articles, but when they do, they get upset. And you can agree that people hate it—given the dozens of e-mails, phone calls, and complaining street chats you are accosted with."

"I love that," Dana said, nodding. "And the book comes out right around our anniversary, so I can complain about it myself at our anniversary party."

"Perfect." I kiss her. "The perfect wife."

VI.

ESCAPE FROM
THE UPPER EAST SIDE

19. BICOASTAL CURRENCY

Fame Versus Money

"IT TRULY IS A MASTERPIECE," I stated, as I retrieved my horn-rimmed reading glasses from my handkerchief pocket and spied the '60s Warhol, dazzled by the monochromatic pigments. It had found its way onto the paneled wall of one of the great private Beaux-Arts mansions between Madison and Fifth Avenues.

"I am really happy for you." I patted my friend's shoulder, congratulating him on being able to acquire one of the great pieces of twentieth-century art in such a highly competitive market.

"Thank you. We really are very excited," he said, beaming. "And to top it off, it has great *provenance*." He revealed the prior owner's name, widely considered one of the century's great financial geniuses and collectors, and whose name and reputation alone add to the buyers' premium. "I never thought I'd have a [type of iconic Warhol], and I never thought it would have come from the Steinhauser (not the real name) collection," he said, exhibiting collector's reverie. Just knowing that the painting graced the Steinhauser manse had me guesstimating as to how much *more* he actually paid for it, although it would be listed on Artnet later that month if I really wanted to snoop.

The following Tuesday I found myself having an alfresco lunch on the terrace of one of the great iconic Malibu beach homes, hosted by one of LA's premier power couples. A famous TV producer and his boyfriend were guests in residence and were stylishly turned out in James Perse's Malibu beachwear complemented by chic straw '50s chapeaux. The waves were cresting as we ate freshly assembled salads direct from the Malibu Mart and watched the towheaded children straddling their boards in the distance. In a case of mistaken (upscale) packaging identity, the wife inadvertently poured soap on her husband's salad from a bottle resembling olive oil.

"What, are you trying to poison me to get the real estate?" he choked.

"Oh, no!" She laughed in a horrified fashion, picking up the bottle of liquid soap. "Everything out here looks like it's straight from Tuscany," she said, picking up and showing us the soap bottle, which had the same green glass and quill-pen-style typography of a high-end estate olive oil.

"This house is truly a masterpiece." I changed the subject as she remade and redressed her husband's salad with real virgin oil from another, but similar bottle she plucked from the pantry. I looked around and marveled at the distinctive '60s architecture, which often appears on book covers.

"Yes, we are very lucky," the sexy blond LA Hollywood wife remarked. "My father-in-law was smart enough to have bought it from [a MAJOR '70s rock star]. Every time I run into his ex-wife [former, major Hollywood wife], she tells me she is so sorry to have sold it in the divorce. The walls must have seen a lot in their day." She winked; images of '70s hair, spandex, and half-naked, gyrating groupies floated through my head. That said, the house took on a sexier allure, now that I knew that the *über*famous blond rocker previously owned it. Rock Superstar provenance is as good at it gets in LA.

What serves as provenance clearly differs between financially based New York and fame-based LA. While certainly not a new topic and one that has been long documented in film, TV, and literature, the divide between the coasts has become more palpable. Economics often bring things to a head, and the cultures have grown more distinct with people on each coast eyeing one another more suspiciously than in the past. Fame versus money can be a potent argument.

"I would NEVER raise my children in Los *Angeles*." Park Avenue Matron sniffed, pronouncing the word with a clear disdain in reaction to a friend who had just relayed the news that a New York couple, who had moved there, was filing for divorce. I was standing at a Mecox Bay cocktail party catching up with some friends, overlooking the purple sunset from the bay to the ocean and declining fattening hors d'oeuvres from the dashing cater waiter staff.

"And why is that?" I said with clear interest.

"I don't even want *him* going there on business," she said, talking about her Lilliputian but Legendary Hedge Fund Manager husband. He was standing there silently, in a sheepish fashion. "It's just not good for a marriage," she declared, the other women gathering around nodding in agreement.

"And why would that be? There are plenty of happily married people in LA," I offered.

"Are there?" Park Avenue Matron asked, her temperature rising as she adjusted her cashmere sweater set. "Name them. All I know is that whenever someone I know moves to LA, six months later the husband meets an actress or a porn star. Or worse, goes over to the *other side*."

"Other side?"

"What do they call it? The velvet mafia?"

"So you think affairs and sexuality are location based?" I asked.

"Richard, don't get cute with me."

"I'm not," I said, somewhat flushed. "I am not being funny. It's just, I'm writing an article and wanted to know what people think."

"Well, I just told you. I think LA has no morals and I would never raise my children there. So they can turn out like so-and-so and so-and-so." She harrumphed and listed the progeny from two well-regarded and name-brand families—where the well-known children have clearly spotty reputations.

"Now that you mention it, I can see your point." I nodded, thinking of the possibility of circulating porn tapes and oft-reported drunken brawls.

"The problem is that LA is all about fame, and people will do anything to get it. Anything." She sounded as if she were Aimee Semple McPherson preaching to the faithful.

"Is this restriction against LA socializing limited to living there or does it also include visiting?"

"We sometimes stop off at the Beverly Hills Hotel before we fly off to Punta Mita or Hawaii. I can abide a day or two, but he's *NOT ALLOWED* to go to bars and restaurants by himself."

"Is he allowed to go out to business dinners and trips in New York?"

"Of course he is," she stated.

"And why is that?"

"Because no one is really *interested* in him in New York," she said with the utmost seriousness. "The really pretty ones here want unattached, *real money* and aren't that interested in someone with four children in private school." She went on approvingly, "Everyone knows the economics in New York, especially the younger girls. You can get a house with a pool for virtually nothing in LA, but everyone knows how expensive New York apartments are. Even if one's rich. Family baggage is too expensive for the pretty young things."

"And LA?"

"From what I hear, they'll go out with anyone if the man buys them a new set of boobs or can lease them a Mercedes."

"So I take it USC or UCLA will not be on your children's radar for college."

"Why would they want to go *there*, when they will be perfectly happy at Penn?" She reached for a pig in a blanket.

"I see your point. Although I hear the girls are prettier at Miami," I joked, knowing she has college-age boys.

"Just what I need. A daughter-in-law from LA or . . . heaven help me, from *Miami*. I'd rather commit hari-kari." And with that she walked away, looking for her husband, who somehow had disappeared.

"LA is really about what your last project was or your next one is," Resort Friend told me. (A resort friend is someone you see and are friendly with on vacations at resorts but don't see during the year.) Resort Friend, a native New Yorker, had moved his NY-based family to LA to work for an investment bank. I called RF to catch up and reached him on the phone in his car, which is where he spends a disproportionate amount of his day.

"Did I get you at a bad time?" I asked from my landline in New York.

"No. This is great. I'm in traffic on the freeway," he reported from the gridlock.

"How much time do you spend in your car?"

"Too much. It's really one of the only issues I have with LA."

"I know," I empathized. "If I had to write an advertising tagline slogan for LA it would be 'it's great when you finally get where you're going.'"

I heard the honking of horns in the background.

"So how has it been now that you're living there? Are you guys loving it?" I asked.

"I really do. I love the weather, and it's so much less stress than New York. Except for the traffic and the smog and some of the people."

"What are the major differences?"

"LA really is about what your next project is and New York is really about what your next purchase is. So LA is about outdoing your friends from a project POV and New York is about outspending your neighbor with purchases. My experience has been New York is all about the money culture. And it's only getting worse."

"So do you find yourself more or less interesting to people because you're not in entertainment in LA?"

"It varies. Some people really enjoy speaking to someone different and they are interested in how to invest—so there are those people who think I'm *more* interesting. That said, there are some people in the entertainment grid who *only* want to talk about the industry and have no patience for anyone who is not involved. I'd be a waste of their time because I'm not a stepping-stone to their next project or movie."

"Do you find that in LA fame is a currency like money?"

"Absolutely." I heard a screech. "Sorry, a car just almost side-swiped me. You have to understand, when you're talking about famous in LA you're talking about *really famous*. So if I go to the school baseball game at [prestigious LA private school] and I'm hanging with the dads, the paparazzi could be waiting outside the field. It's no big deal to me."

"And your wife?"

"I think she cares a bit more about going to industry parties. You know, the red carpet events."

"So she likes the fame game?"

"I think so. And she thinks it would be good for her business."

"Business? I thought she was a homemaker?"

"She is, but she's writing a screenplay and wants to direct."

"Celebrity has traditionally worked against the real estate process in New York, which is why celebs used to be relegated to living on Central Park West," Ageless Real Estate Broker commented, pointing out the window of the chauffeur-driven Mercedes. "Marco, can you take us down to the Dakota?" She again pointed a perfectly lacquered fingernail.

"Not a bad place to camp out," I observed.

"Up until a few years ago most co-ops on Fifth Avenue wouldn't accept actors," she said with a sniff. She reeled off a list of superstars who were all turned down by tony Fifth and Park Avenue buildings, including one of the most famous leading men of the 1970s, who was turned down at the building I actually live in.

"The West Side was always more accepting of creative people," she commented.

"I just read a quote attributed to Lauren Bacall where she said 'New York was far more interesting when it just wasn't about the money.'"

"I'm sure it was. That's why she lived in the Dakota. It always accepted the most fabulous show people: Baryshnikov, John Lennon of course. I'm trying to get the listing for her apartment. I hear it is coming on the market . . . somewhere in the twenty-six-million-dollar range," she speculated. "So she did very well for herself despite what she said."

"Why do you think celebrities are shunned at East Side co-ops?"

"Richard, don't be naive. I once tried to sell a major celebrity superstar an apartment from an old line heiress on Fifth Avenue. I said, 'You must meet so-and-so; she really is fabulous and she's one of the major singers of her generation,' trying to impress the old witch."

"And what did she say?" I asked.

"She said, 'Darling, don't even have her come by. Firstly, I have no idea who she is. I haven't ever heard a song she's sung. Secondly, I would never ever sell my apartment to her. We don't associate with *show people.*' "

"And what happened?"

"The star wouldn't listen and put in her offer and board package, and it was promptly turned down."

"Where did she end up moving?"

"The West Side, of course. New York doesn't care how famous you are. The women in the building also didn't want her around their husbands. It's a story as old as time. Not that the celeb would have wanted a seventy-five-year-old investment banker."

"And what about so-and-so?" I referenced the leading man. "Why would my building have turned someone like him down?" (He had an elegant image.)

"Most of the old geezers don't want press outside their door. They also don't want to look bad in front of their wives. That said, they did let [THE MOST FAMOUS AMERICAN MALE MOVIE STAR] buy the penthouse duplex of your building."

"Yes, of course." I remembered seeing the iconic blond star in the elevator, and my mother-in-law almost fainting at the sight of him.

"How did *he* get in?"

"He was known as the handsomest man of his generation. Really, I believe he is the one star who could live on Fifth Avenue."

"And why is that?"

"Because he's the only man every woman wanted to sleep with and every man want to *be*. Other than that . . . It's the West Side, baby," she said as she instructed Marco to turn onto Central Park South.

"Houses are also celebrities in LA." Eileen Graybar (not her real name), an older female TV star, brought me a mug of coffee in the chic house she had just renovated in the Hollywood Hills. A standard in TV and Movie of the Week classics, where she was known for being able to pull off both *perky* and *evil* simultaneously, this former ingénue is now known for her chic taste and business savvy. When the roles started to dry up, she turned her creative energy toward buying, renovating, and flipping homes. I looked around at the beautiful Mediterranean architecture and casual LA décor that appeals: all creams, beiges, and chenille.

She filled me in: "Houses are known by the stars who have lived in them, but in Beverly Hills and Bel Air some of the great estates are also famous. If you told someone you bought the Beach Crest (not its real name) on Loma Vista and you're *not famous*, people would assume you'd have to be a tech company billionaire or a Middle Eastern potentate."

"Do the stars still live in those grand estates?" I asked.

"Only a handful. The celebrities have been outpriced by the international billionaires like everyone else. But you still see the maps of the celebrity homes being sold and the tour buses. I'm only talking about the truly remarkable estates. Some have been torn down and subdivided, but there are still a few that exist and trade hands."

"Where do most of the big stars live today?"

"Well, in this town it all depends on whether you're on the *ascent* or the *descent*. Two or three big movies and an Oscar nomination and you might live in Brentwood or Holmby Hills. Then you have a flop or two and you sell your mansion and move to the flats. When you lose your teeth, you live in a condo in Westwood."

"That's a hard reality." I coughed.

"Most celebs get bad financial advice and think it's never going to end. They think they are invincible and the roles will always keep coming." She went on ruefully and with a knowing expression, "And they end up spending their money on clothes, cars, boats, watches. Try and sell all those things when you need the cash and see how much you get."

"How did you get into the real estate business?"

"I got smarter." She suddenly looked both perky and then evil as she pulled her knees toward her on the big LA sectional, and her green eyes caught the light.

"When I started losing ingénue roles to younger girls, I was still getting work as the older sister, so I wasn't worried. A few years later when I started getting sent up for the mother roles, I started to panic. Then one day I walked into a casting and they said 'Nice meeting you but we told your agent *not* to have you come. We told Sid we're looking for an Eileen Graybar type, not Eileen Graybar!!!!'"

"That's surreal." I sipped my coffee.

"It's a true story. I went home, had a good cry, and called a friend of mine." She mentioned an older former star who pulled off a haul on a few ex-husbands. "She said to me, 'Eileen, the only thing that's constant in this town is the sun, the sex, and the real estate.' The next day I decided to go for my real estate license and I've made more money in real estate than I ever did in residuals."

"Congratulations. The house is beautiful and I'm so happy you made out so well in the end."

"Well, the money is good and I live very well, but . . ." She paused. "I just need to find my comeback role. You know," she said wistfully, "once you have had a bit of fame, nothing else seems to matter." She sighed. "More coffee?"

"Reality TV has cheapened celebrity." The Octogenarian, Old-school Agent spoke to me off the record at Michael's, the media dining room where most things are *on* the record, including who's eating there and what table they occupy.

"When I first got into the business, if you were famous, you were famous because you *did* something. You were a great method actor. You were a dashing leading man or a musical star. You had to *do* something to be a star."

His comment reminded me of a quote I'd read about the famous 1940s aquatic star Esther Williams. "It's like Fanny Brice said about Esther Williams," I offered. " 'Wet she's a star. Dry, she ain't.' "

"Exactly, but once Esther got in the water she really was a star."

"I can actually attest to seeing her in her later years doing laps in the pool at the Villa d'Este," I recalled.

"And?"

"And wet she was a star . . ." I remembered her graceful, ageless strokes.

The agent went on, "In my day you had to go to LA for TV and film, and stars came to New York to do Broadway. Or if they were famous singers, we would book them into club dates in the best venues in New York. Even Vegas had an elegance to it."

"How do you think that has affected Los Angeles versus New York culture?"

"In the '60s, '70s, if someone in New York was known to be a millionaire, which was a big thing in those days, they came from a credible fortune. Or if they were a star in LA, they were a star, not a reality star. Today, everyone gives the appearance of having money or fame. Then you find out it's all stolen or they made it in an unsavory way or they're living off credit cards with a rented Bentley."

"Can you elaborate?" I asked.

"Yes. Perhaps the way to describe it would be to say they have reality-show money versus real money," he remarked in a droll fashion, his graceful filigree cuff links glittering in the perfectly starched and ironed Charvet cuffs. After a moment he said, toying with his chicken paillard, "I do feel sorry for you all."

"Why is that?"

"It was so much more fun when it was *real*."

As the summer was coming to a close, Dana and I stopped by my sister's chic beach cottage in Amagansett for a lively lunch on her deck, the sounds of the ocean in the distance somewhat operatic in scale. Her dear friends Kurt and his husband, Danny, a transplanted LA couple, joined. (Kurt, an entertainment executive, had moved to

New York when Danny became the principal of a prestigious New York private school.)

"There's nothing better than smoked salmon for a real 'New Yawk' Sunday brunch." My sister offered the salmon platter. "Yum." I offered Kurt the salmon. "Did you find living in LA all about fame?"

"Yes, because people *live off* the proximity to fame in LA. If you are in real estate, a home is advertised as a 'star's compound' in the hills to help market it; a salon gets business by doing a popular actress's hair and makeup. In New York, everything has to stand on its own merits. Does the salon actually do good work? Does the apartment or house actually have good bones? LA is *tainted* by fame!"

"But did you like living in LA?" I asked, knowing I had a live one in my clutches.

"I mean, it *is* fabulous. The best thing about LA is that it has a sense of *possibility*. It has that 'I'm going to make it overnight' thing. Someone can be living out of a rented car, write a screenplay, go to a club, meet an agent, and then they're accepting an Oscar and it happens for them. New York is much more serious and stratified."

"Do you feel differently in LA versus New York?"

"Yes, one can definitely live a lot better in LA on less money." He laughed. "And you can be a poseur in LA for *a lot* less."

"How so?" I was intrigued.

"Well, you can totally front it; you have your rented car, you can be crashing at your friend's apartment and have a business card made up that says you're a 'producer.' People aren't that smart in LA. In New York they look around and can do the math on who you are and how much your co-op costs. And everyone knows if you are actually living *in* a co-op, the board vetted you and that you had to have *real* money to buy it. It's a much harder nut to crack in New York. You're really locked out unless you're the one percent. In LA, they can't even do the math." He shrugged. "Additionally, I think LA currency is about the body, and New York currency is the mind."

"How so?" I asked.

"There's little or no pedigree in LA. In New York, age and experience promise bigger job titles, money; when you or your family have earned it, you have pedigree. Everyone in New York idolized [famous timeless socialite who reached the age of one hundred]. No one in LA is a hundred years old and no one has pedigree, so better to act young and be young. Age has no benefit in LA. Although everyone in LA respects the culture of intelligence in New York."

"So youth and beauty in LA are your ticket to fame."

Kurt nodded and seemed to enjoy the sunshine and lay back in his director's chair soaking up rays like a Persian cat.

"And how has New York been for you versus your years as a producer in LA?" I asked.

"Well, when we were living in LA, if we went to a party, as an example, people used to take me seriously and I was definitely in the mix. On the other hand, Danny said people used to look right past him when they asked him what he did and found out he was a teacher."

"That's a shame," I sympathized.

"And now we live in New York and people say to me, 'Oh dear, you're in *entertainment*,' and pay me no mind and focus on Danny."

"Why's that?" I leaned in.

"Because," he said, sipping his sauvignon blanc, "they find out he's one of the heads of the [elite NYC private school] and they all want him to help get their kids into school."

"That's New York for you," I acknowledged.

One humid evening back in Manhattan, the Silver Fox and his paramour, L'actrice, picked me up in their delightfully air-conditioned SUV and we drove to Midtown for dinner. Dana was out of town, and I welcomed the company. I hadn't seen L'actrice since Capri, and she filled me in on her latest role in a movie directed by one of the most famous comedic actresses of the '80s, who will go down in movie history for a comedic scene in a deli. I told her about my book deal and the piece that I was writing on LA versus New York currency.

As L'actrice looked into her Chanel compact, she paraphrased a quote by the wonderful playwright Neil Simon. "I think it sums up your piece, Richard. He said that whether it's one hundred degrees or thirty degrees in New York, in Los Angeles it's always seventy-two. Yet there are six million interesting people in New York and just seventy-two in Los Angeles."

20. THE EMPTONS

Estates Sit Empty as Longtime Hamptonians Flee for European Shores

IT WAS OPENING WEEKEND in the Hamptons.

There I was at a Memorial Day party at a stunning manse "on Goldman Pond," as some now refer to the body of water formerly known as Sagg Pond. Now home to some of the most expensive waterfront Hamptons properties, it has become a coveted location for deep-pocketed financial-industry types in search of deepwater docks.

I was air-kissing couples dressed optimistically in nautical blue and white despite the persistent rain.

"Great to see you, Richard," a friend's taut wife said with a smile.

After a brief exchange in a mist of orange-blossom fragrance, everyone was saying their thank-yous to the evening's host and hostess, along with their good-byes.

"See you in August." She smiled.

"Where are you off to?"

"Antibes."

"And you?" I questioned a lingering neighbor.

"Sardinia. It's a family tradition," she explained. "See you in late July."

"See you in August," I said to a friend.

"Have fun in Saint-Tropez!" he echoed.

"Have fun in Capri!"

"Have fun in Mykonos." We all hugged.

"Are you out here for Thanksgiving?" a summer friend asked, walking us out of the party. "That's the next time we'll be here. Let's put something on the calendar for the fall."

It was only the first weekend, and the Hamptons' early-summer exodus had begun.

While some friends remain passionate about the surfing lessons, the $100-a-pound lobster salad (from you know where), and the purple-streaked Sagaponack sunsets, there is a distinct group of people using their Hamptons estates less and less, with no plans either to sell or rent. "Whole neighborhoods are on timers," said a busy housesitter I ran into in the local hardware store. "At nine fifteen, it lights up like the Christmas tree at Rockefeller Center."

As Dana and I were driving home from the party, we passed by a neighbor's house, a recently assembled McMansion with turreted peaks and outsize turn-of-the-century demilune windows.

"Have you ever met them?" Dana asked me.

I recalled popping by with a bottle of French rosé when the couple first moved in. "Yeah," I said, "when I took over the housewarming gift."

"I've never met them." She shrugged, turning onto our property. "It's a *little* weird, given they bought the house five years ago and they live only a few houses down."

"I like a quiet neighborhood," I said.

"Fine, but if you run into them, tell them that they need to reset their light timer," she said. "They forgot it's no longer daylight savings time."

It all seemed to jell for me in the first-class lounge at Kennedy, where we bumped into three couples en route to different European locales.

"We bolt the moment we drop the kids off at the camp buses in front of the Met. I give a good cry, and then we make a mad dash for the airport," a friend's wife said, snagging a complimentary foil packet of peanuts and a mimosa before offering me a Xanax from the pill case in her zippered Vuitton makeup bag. "The kids aren't allowed to call for ten days anyway, so it's a guilt-free getaway," she remarked as she started to drift off into a blissful repose.

"Where are you off to?" I asked as she gulped back her little helper.

"Saint-Tropez. And you?" she managed to ask.

"Capri."

"Well, you might as well have never left the beach club," she cackled as she rattled off a dozen or so couples leaving their Hamptons abodes to make a pilgrimage to the Amalfi Coast.

She wasn't wrong. The following day, I was in the Piazza di Spagna, making my way to the Caffè Greco Antico for an afternoon espresso, when I ran into a popular Hamptonite and his wife, their designer shopping bags overflowing with VAT envelopes and satin-ribboned boxes wrapped as only the Italians can.

"My children have no desire to go to the Hamptons anymore. We used to go every weekend when they were younger. Now they want to be with their friends in the city." He paused. "So we just go to the Med."

"Why not sell it, then?" I prompted.

"No. They would be too upset. They like to know it's there . . . the way she likes to know her engagement ring is in the safe but only wears it two times a year."

"Honey, come over here," his wife motioned excitedly, peering into the window of one of Italy's most exclusive jewelry stores.

"I like Italy or France in the summer. I can get away from all the boiler and air-conditioner and basement mold problems—not to mention the roof, or not being able to get in touch with my decorator. It's actually cheaper if I buy her a pair of those earrings than if we were in Bridge and she wanted to start a redecorating project."

"Well, have a great Fourth."

"You too. Have fun in Capri. Don't mention my name in any of the shops, or they may charge you extra," he said, laughing good-naturedly.

My late father used to say that staying in a five-star hotel without any luggage is the ultimate luxury. That said, staying in a heralded European resort does not even cut the *moutarde* for some Hamptons elites.

My wife and I were having an intimate lunch at La Fontelina, one of Capri's best and most picturesque seaside kitchens, when a group of familiar faces alighted from a cruise-ship-size yacht in the distance.

"Enjoying yourselves?" I asked as they occupied the table next to ours.

"What's not to enjoy on two hundred and twenty-five feet?" A Southampton fixture shrugged with self-satisfaction.

"Fantastico," one of the wives exclaimed, her newly acquired laminates glimmering like pearlized reflectors.

"Oh, you're *just* in a hotel?" she sympathized. "Next time you must do a *ship*! We sleep like babies, and the best thing is, we wake up in Portofino or Croatia—not the North Fork."

"So who's in the Hamptons house?" I asked.

"I give it to my in-laws," the husband revealed. "This way they're taken care of and I don't have to see them."

"It's the gift that keeps on giving," he went on, guffawing as he dipped into a platter of fried calamari.

"I really hate the Hamptons," I heard one of the wives say as we stood to leave.

"So sell it," someone said.

"Well, I'm certainly not going to sell it and go somewhere I would *never use* like the Jersey Shore." She mentioned her friends who recently bought in Connecticut. "It's like being in an old-age home in the forest. Nothing to do or buy. Just dead leaves everywhere."

In the chic, potted garden of the Hotel de Russie, an acquaintance recounted his long path to Hamptons estate ownership, along with its recent disappointments.

"When I was in my twenties, I did the typical share house in Quogue where you could put your fist through the Sheetrock," he told me.

"I got married and then a promotion and we bought our first house, north of the highway, on a cul-de-sac. When I finally made a real bonus, we bought a house in the promised land *south of the highway* in Bridgehampton, with farm views."

"And then?" I asked, plying him with prosecco and olives.

"Once we bought the big house, my wife got to hire a real decorator. Guess what?"

"What?" I leaned in.

"We invited our friends over for a party in July."

"And?"

"And no one was in town." He wiped his forehead. "It's crazy; we spent all this time and money, and no one was home."

"Well," the wife added, "it would still be better if we were on the ocean or the pond. Maybe they'd come *then*."

Another couple I had drinks with on the terrace of the Grand Hotel Quisisana barely use their house in the estate section of Southampton—but are nevertheless considering upgrading to oceanfront. "I only use my house two days a year," the husband said between puffs of a cigar. "My wife is mostly at our house in Aspen. What do I need a huge house for, when we can sell it and upgrade to the ocean, even if it's only six or seven thousand square feet?"

"So you can go for five days instead of two?" I joked.

"How did you know?" he said in all seriousness.

As it turns out, getting a bigger house to not stay in appears to be something of a trend among Hamptons evacuees. The next day, Dana and I had an alfresco lunch with one of the Hamptons' most stylish hostesses and her husband. As the bread basket arrived, she reached into her beach bag and produced a package of low-cal GG crackers. "We go away to be together," remarked her husband, a well-regarded CEO of a public company, "and escape the social pressure of the Hamptons."

The wife munched on the cracker with some marinated eggplant. "While we may only spend thirty days a year there, I view owning a

Hamptons property as part of a diversified real estate portfolio," she said. "And as far as I'm concerned, 11962 is the *primest*."

Toasting over a pitcher of sangria, the husband added, "When I'm buying a business today, I look at EBITA—earnings before interest, tax, and amortization. When it comes to owning a home in the Hamptons, it's EBITFV, earnings before interest, taxes, and family values. You can't put a price on it. As the kids get older, they come back—and that's when they want a bigger house."

"Suddenly your kids have a boyfriend or girlfriend in tow and not a nanny," she chimed in.

"So you're looking for a bigger place?" I stirred the pot.

"Of course," she answered. "Can I be honest? It's time for a *frickin' upgrade*."

"We want three chimneys, like every other partner on Wall Street!" He laughed.

John Paul Getty's converted seaside palazzo isn't exactly a shabby place to end a vacation before dealing with the lines at Fiumicino Airport. During hors d'oeuvres on the gorgeous outdoor candlelit terrace, the pianist played soothing Chopin études.

As guests arrived for drinks, I spied a familiar ace on the Hamptons circuit talking on the phone in the no-cell-phone area while pacing the seawall.

"There's nothing like Italy and France in July," he said into the phone. "No, they couldn't come this year. Yeah, it's a shame. They stayed home and had to use their house in the Hamptons. I guess he didn't have a great year."

I wasn't sure whom he was talking about, but the conversation couldn't be ignored.

"Maybe they'll be able to come next year," he said, choosing a quail-egg-size green olive. "Although I'm not sure where I'll be. I hear Sun Valley is really great in the summer."

21. STRESSMAS VACATION

Trying to Relax Without a Lounge Chair, Dinner Reservation, or Tennis Slot

IT HAD BEEN MANY YEARS since I'd been to an event on the St. Regis rooftop, the last one being my very own wedding to Dana, oh so many moons ago. It was a balmy afternoon this past October when we returned to celebrate a dear friend's family event at an elegant luncheon. We once again found ourselves in the Fabergé-style ballroom, which by day felt like being on the set of *The Prince and the Showgirl*, although Olivier was not in attendance.

The conversation at our table turned to the holidays. I leaned in to talk with a formidable businessman who is as smart as he is efficient. "And what are your plans?" I asked, taking a taste of the silky mousseline.

He mentioned a well-known island resort.

"Have you been there before?" I inquired.

"It's our fourth year, which helps."

"Helps? How so?" My ears perked up.

"Everything is booked a year in advance. If you want your rooms, your tennis, your restaurant reservations, spa services, you have to do it all the *moment* it opens up. My secretary calendarizes it," he explained.

As his chic and engaging wife returned to the table and placed her minaudière next to her setting, she smiled knowingly while picking up her mimosa.

"Remember when we used to go to Anguilla year after year, and when Giorgio (not his real name) would come to New York, everyone would rush to take him out to Cipriani and Elios?" she recalled.

"Who is Giorgio?" I asked.

"Giorgio was head of the pool and beachfront, and if you wanted the best lounge chair setups in the prime location, you needed to butter him up." She smiled sagely.

"Giorgio sounds like one lucky guy."

"We took him out to Sette Mezzo, but the so-and-sos went to the next level—dinner *and* a cashmere sweater from Bergdorf. *They* got the prime spot and cabana the next year." She sighed.

"This actually happened?"

"Don't be naïve. It's all a year in advance and about greasing palms," she said, munching on an asparagus tip. "Or you get nothing, darling, positively *nothing*."

Whether it's escaping the northeast for St. Barths, Anguilla, Aspen, or Miami, it always appeared that the vacations were stressful until you got there. Now it's worse when you arrive. Perhaps the greatest misconception of all surrounding the holidays is that it is actually a *vacation*.

"You spend half your net worth getting wherever you're going," a good friend said over tequila and orange slices in front of his crackling fireplace. "And then when you finally get to the resort, you're tired and hungry, and you check with the front desk for a reservation. The concierge says, 'It's *all booked* for dinner,' and they have *nothing* available."

"This actually happened?" I said.

"Of course."

"What did you do?"

"I complained, and they finally set up a table for us for dinner—in the lobby," he said.

An erudite advertising executive had this to say over a lubricated *Mad Men*–style working lunch at Circo: "It's not a vacation, it's an emotional reckoning." He swirled his glass of La Scolca Gavi di Gavi. "You're told to be happy and to relax, and *that's* what creates the stress. It's the idea that it should be wonderful. You're supposed to be joyous and thankful, and when you ask yourselves those questions, you come up short. . . . Do you think we can order another bottle?"

Besides in-law and family stress—"My in-laws command everyone to eat at five thirty, and since they're paying . . ."—the number one complaint among those I spoke to was not being able to secure a well-situated lounge chair, if any at all, without having to shell out thousands. "How can I be spending all that money on a vacation and not have a place to sit?" was a common refrain. The idea of having to set an alarm to save a lounge chair seemed to rile everyone, while stretches of chairs staked out with Havaianas, month-old magazines, sunglasses, and paperbacks sent people into veritable fits.

"It's absolutely ridiculous," a Park Avenue matron said at the bar at Sant Ambroeus. I had stopped in for an afternoon espresso while she was ordering a Negroni.

"I shouldn't have to tip to get a lounge chair. It *should* be included! You have these people saving twelve lounge chairs at a time; no one uses them, and then the moment you try and take one, suddenly an angry housewife from New Jersey appears and screams, 'It's taken!' like a skunk marking its territory. That's the *main reason* we bought the house in Palm Beach. It's well located with a pool and beach access, but best of all, I have six *glorious* lounge chairs awaiting me each and every day, and they're all *mine*, M-I-N-E," she said like a woman possessed, her vintage Verdura cuffs raised in a victory sign.

"If you're going to succeed, you have to have a *system*," a curvaceous social powerhouse said over dinner at the Mark. "Really, it's all about communication and tipping."

"So what's your secret to success?" I queried, sampling the tuna tartare.

"If you choose to go to a hotel or resort over Christmas, you have to make yourself known and *early*."

"Meaning?"

"Before I even unpack my bags, I go down to the pool and find the *main* guy."

"How do you find the main guy, and how much does it take to succeed?"

"The main guy is always the busiest with the most *expensive* sunglasses. Whereas people in the States tip at the *end*, I tip before. Of course, I ask if he's going to be there tomorrow, because why tip someone who's going on a day off?"

"She has her system down pat." Her tycoon husband beamed.

"I might give him a hundred-dollar bill the first day. Then I get the six lounge chairs, umbrellas, the romaine and shrimp cocktail set up, sparkling water, of course all before lunch. Then I might still give one hundred dollars the next day and gradually start handing out fifties."

"Her system works," the husband marveled. "And don't forget the tennis time. The prime slot is eight. Seven is too early, and nine is too hot."

"That's all well and good," she said, sipping a white wine spritzer. "But a good vacation is all about a great lounge setup with your girlfriends and great people watching."

Some resorts have started to restrict seating to only one lounge chair per guest and one umbrella per every two chairs. Many New York vacationers feel it's long overdue.

"There was a family I knew who many years ago went to Mexico on a vacation, and their parents and another family's parents got into a fistfight over lounge chairs," a childhood friend said over dinner. "Many years later, the daughter got engaged, and both sets of in-laws were going to meet for the first time."

"And?" I said with bated breath.

"And when they met, it was the same two families!"

"What happened?" I said, taking some of the gigande beans and marouli salad.

"They actually called off the wedding!"

"No, that must be an *urban* legend!" I said emphatically.

"Perhaps in New York, but not in *Scarsdale*," she explained, sipping her sauvignon blanc.

Later that week, I was having lunch with a well-known television executive at Michael's, where chicken paillard, a table in the epicenter, and a visit from Michael himself anoints one as a member of the media elite. The executive himself, who is extremely funny and observant, has been on the vacation circuit for many years with his family and has navigated the rough seas of holiday vacation planning.

"The arms race for the holiday season has begun," he declared. "It's not just the choosing availability; these days, it seems there's *itinerary competition* on who can go to the most arcane and far-flung places. The children all talk to each other: 'I'm going on safari, I'm going to the rain forest, I'm seeing the Great Wall.'"

"Around the world in eight days," I said.

"At this point, in order to go somewhere different, I'd have to tell people I'm taking my children to the green line in Iraq," he said.

"Most of the kids I see on vacation are texting the whole time anyway," I offered, thinking back to historic locations and visions of uninterested children, eyes glued to their devices instead of the monumental landmarks.

All this talk put a damper on my holiday mood until I took my sister, Susan, and her husband, Rob, out for dinner at Elio's to celebrate her birthday. As we were toasting her over chicken scarpariello and fried zucchini, my sister explained her point of view.

"We're just going to the beach house for the holiday," she said, referencing her small but extremely chic beach cottage. "We'll bundle up, light a fire. We'll take a beach walk on New Year's Day."

"Sounds divine," Dana said.

"And then when it's over, I'll just open the car door and drive back to the city."

"That's better than standing in line to take off your shoes and put your laptop in a plastic tray," I said, thinking of our own 6:30 a.m. holiday flight.

"You know," she said, "we just don't travel over the Christmas and New Year's holidays anymore. It's way too stressful. The weather's really not great in the Caribbean or Florida, and why do I want to see all those people you see in New York? But you all can!"

I motioned the waiter over. "Can you bring me a refill?" I pointed to my martini glass.

"Don't worry, Richard," my wife said, patting my hand. "Maybe after it's all over, we can plan a weekend ordering in Chinese food, watching *Homeland*, and having a *real* vacation."

"Let's book it now," I pleaded. "So I have something to look forward to—after the trip."

22. BLING VERSUS THE BONG

St. Barths Versus Jamaica—and
What It Says About You

FRAMED TECHNICOLOR IMAGES of the speldiferous Ursula Andress in her iconic white bikini, attendant conch knife, and the swarthy Sean Connery from the Bond classic *Dr. No* greet guests on the way to dinner at the divine GoldenEye, Chris Blackwell's Caribbean five-star fantasy on Jamaica's remote and lush north coast. The movie was filmed in Jamaica and made the blond bombshell an international star, not to mention my friend Chris very happy, although he doesn't fully kiss and tell.

I had arrived in Jamaica for an advertising shoot for my aviation client, Wheels Up. Chris, my partner and namesake in Blackwell Fine Jamaican Rum and a Wheels Up aficionado, had agreed to appear in the advertising campaign we were shooting at the Ian Fleming International Airport. Chris generously hosted a pre-shoot dinner at his outdoor restaurant, which occupies a promontory overlooking the treetops, a suspension bridge, and the secluded beachfront crescent in the distance. The cicadas were background music to the vintage reggae, and we could easily imagine we were on safari or in the jungles of East Asia as we sat alfresco sampling fresh spiced snapper and pineapple rice and hot fluffy rolls with three types of flavored homemade butter.

Jamaica conjures . . . but GoldenEye, the former home of Ian Fleming, inspires.

Chris, the mastermind behind keeping GoldenEye the Caribbean's chicest and most low-key, barefoot resort, greeted a few under-the-radar and sophisticated guests. I call them *hippies with a bank book*; there's always an assortment of dressed-down movie and rock stars and smart, European couples who *read actual books* on the beach. Dinner is always a quiet affair, without the boisterous and often grotesque behavior on display at other Caribe resorts . . . where men in loud silk shirts quarrel about the location of their tables.

"We have a group of [Iron Curtain potentates] arriving next week," Chris said, sighing at the thought, his Harrovian accent deflecting a bit of disappointment. "I'm certain they won't like it," he said in the concerned tone of an honest parent.

"What will they do here?" a chic Italian ex-pat asked, frowning at the idea, unable to process their arrival or their intention.

"I'm not sure. But they most definitely will not like it," he said in his soft, clipped voice.

"Why is that?" I asked, knowing the answer all too well.

"There's not enough *bling* for them."

Dana and I had agreed to a dinner a few months earlier and met the couple at the bar of an overcrowded UES Italian standard where they keep guests waiting, although one has a solid reservation. I had wanted to decline the dinner invitation but Dana insisted, letting me know the wife (who was working alongside Dana in a charity) would take offense to too many a declined invite. This would not have been our first.

"Where are you for Christmas vacation?" the husband, a diminutive financier, asked once we were finally seated. His diamond cuff links reflected his wife's ten-carat diamond studs, creating a blinding ray of light directed at the fried zucchini. It was hard to hear above the grating din.

"Where are *you* going?" I asked, knowing Jerome (not his real name) wanted to tell me his itinerary first, as finance men usually do.

"We *always* go St. Barths for Christmas," Jerome boasted. "I always take the [enormously expensive beachfront villa] at [fabled and expensive St. Barths hotel]."

"Jerome always wants to rent a house," the wife declared, her diamond pavé Rolex weighing down her anorexic wrist as she lifted one zucchini stick like a barbell. "I'm just stuffed," she declared, excusing herself from having to eat anything else. "But I always tell him that the house renters are just cheapskates and to ante up for the beachfront hotel suite," she exclaimed.

"How 'bout you all? Where are you going?" Jerome asked.

"Jamaica," I said.

"Jamaica???" He looked a bit horrified "How could you go *there*? I went once and I never went back. I didn't feel safe."

"Why is that?"

"Because there are too many natives."

"As opposed to St. Barths where you only see transplanted French socials on *quatre quatres*?" I countered.

"Yes, that's why I like it," the wife said. "I don't have to feel bad or stay hidden behind walls." She clutched her bag, as if someone from Jamaica were going to snatch it in a cloud of reefer madness.

"I have been going to Jamaica for twenty years, and Dana and I have gone everywhere and we never had a problem. They have had issues with crime in certain areas, but overall, if you are cool with people, they are cool with you. The Jamaican people are the world's nicest people. So lovely."

"We love going down the Martha Brae River on a bamboo raft. They chill Red Stripe in the water and it's supercold," Dana said, smiling at the memory.

"We don't drink beer. Only rosé champagne," Jerome stated without humor.

"And the food is the best. I love jerk anything," Dana soldiered on.

"Jerome can't handle spice. He gets dyspepsia," his wife revealed.

A bit too much information, I thought while envisioning Jerome in the bathroom, agonizing over a jerk snapper.

"Do you actually take your children?" Jerome asked incredulously.

"My kids love it there. I took them to climb Dunn's River Falls and it was out of *Blue Lagoon.*"

"Well, we would never go there," the wife said firmly.

"Different strokes for different folks. I would never go to St. Barths over Christmas vacation." I decided to engage.

"Well, you would if you had our accommodations," Jerome said defensively.

I threw all caution to the wind, sensing a fight.

"Actually, my friend is an investor in the hotel and we would very well get the accommodation if we wanted." I raised an eyebrow at Dana, signaling it was time to get the check.

As we swilled coffee and rose to our feet, we all knew that dinner was a one-time affair. While Jerome was helping his wife on with her chocolate sable chubby, I heard him say, "These people are crazy. Who in our crowd loves *Jamaica?*"

There comes a certain point in your life when taste differentiates. You say *pot*atoes and I say pot*a*toes, but at the end of the day you're either OK with consuming carbs or not. Sometimes in life, there are markers that exist as a filter, a way to sort things out. I have come to view Jamaica love as one such filter, a meter of connection, affiliation, and shared taste. To be truthful, if you prefer France over Italy or St. Barths over Jamaica, chances are we're *not* going to be besties. Of course, there are a few exceptions to the rule. But for the most part, it *ain't* going to happen, mon. You're either a disciple of "the bong" and all that encompasses or you're a slave to "the bling."

"We are definitely separated at birth," one of my closest friends, Jay, declared over organic salmon at the Downtown restaurant we frequent weekly and that I choose not to reveal lest we lose our regular table (and secret dish). The eponymous *über*menswear designer had just returned from a long weekend in Jamaica with his wife. We were bonding over our shared Jamaica experiences as only best friends in our circle could do.

"I saw this awful New York couple going down on the same flight with me." He described a highly annoying couple and their children, and their tedious, pretentious behavior.

"I asked them if they made the wrong flight." He laughed, suggesting to me he thought they may have missed their flight to Ibiza or St. Barths. We both laughed when I told him that given his colorful description, I actually knew who they were. I pulled up a random Google photo, to his delight—and horror.

"I have to have a house there." Jay declared, his serious collection of man bracelets sporting a few new green, black, and yellow woven wristbands. Jay and his wife love GoldenEye, but also favor the dramatic cliffs of Negril.

"The energy in Jamaica is unlike that on any other island I have ever been to." He shrugged. "You feel like when they speak you're listening to music even when they're not singing. There's a constant smell of weed, the water, and Rastas. Overall, I see really happy people."

"It's the one place I go to get my groove back," I add.

"I feel so chill there. Coming from a city where so few people have real style, everyone has style there no matter how much money they have."

"How many times do you go there a year?"

"As many times as I can. It's one hundred percent authentic. Other islands are totally manufactured, trying to appeal to tourists. Jamaica is not manufactured fun."

"What's your favorite thing about it?"

"The people. They appreciate life so much more than any other place I have ever been. They're passionate and also ageless. It's hard to tell how old they are."

"Without plastic surgery à la New York or LA. Why do you think that is?"

"They're different. They're *happy*. They're *high on life*."

There will always be couples who cannot agree on décor or vacation destinations. I have learned the outcome is never pretty.

Dana and I were out with good friends at Orsay, enjoying the *frites*.

"We would love to come with you to Jamaica," the husband—a down-to-earth and good-natured fellow—said as I told them a vacation anecdote.

"GoldenEye is a dream," I said. "We just chill and read, and Dana loves to kayak in the lagoon."

"What about shopping?" the wife said. "Any luxury boutiques?"

"They do have really nice local handmade batik cover-ups," Dana offered. "And a bracelet with a marijuana plant on it."

"I can't go anywhere where they don't have great shopping. That's why I love St. Barths. It has all the best brands," the wife declared.

"Honey, all you do is shop in the same stores in New York and Europe. Maybe it would be good to do something a bit different," the husband chided her.

"Why?" She looked at him like he needed to be checked into a mental institution.

"I'm with Dana. I would like to have an active vacation," he explained.

"Well then, marry *her*! My exercise is using my black card," she stated firmly.

"You actually might like it. The water in the lagoon is aqua," Dana explained. "My favorite thing is to take a shower *au naturel* under the palm tree."

"Wait. There are outdoor bathrooms?" The wife paled. "I like a clean, white marble, indoor bathroom."

"It's really another way to enjoy the incredible nature," Dana said. I looked at the wife and saw this wasn't going to end well.

"The best is you sleep under a net," I said. "It's very *Jungle Book*. But I will say, *it's not for everyone*."

"Sounds amazing," the husband said dreamily.

"A net?????" the wife said in a shrill tone. "No marble bathroom? Why do they need a net?"

"Because you're in a natural environment."

"It says bugs to me. There is NO WAY I AM GOING there." She was becoming apoplectic at the thought.

"Come on, honey. It sounds perfect," the husband said more forcefully as he saw his dreams being dashed before his eyes.

"And every morning, a rooster comes and wakes you up at six a.m. It's like being on a farm near the sea." Dana couldn't help herself at this point.

"A *rooster*? Are you kidding me?" The wife's mouth was agape.

"And only flats; you can't rock your Louboutins on the coral stairs," Dana explained.

"This sounds like my worst nightmare," the wife said.

"We love it, but if it's not for you, you can call [five-star hotel chain where every resort in every country is exactly the same]. We stay there sometimes too. Why rock the boat?" I offered to the husband, not wanting to be the source of a matrimonial dispute.

"Whatever." The husband sighed in a disappointed fashion. "We'll just go to the [five-star chain]. I'll play golf and drink tequila."

The Famous Basketball Star had flown into New York, and Carol, my assistant, had set up drinks with him and one of my lead investors at the taproom in one of New York's most conservative Manhattan clubs. A tie and a blazer are necessary for admittance, and since the Basketball Star is a man of style, I thought he would enjoy a haunt where no jeans or sneakers are allowed. We settled into the paneled room, replete with hunting scenes, faded red leather, and wooden seating. Whiskey and martinis were served by older professional men in white dinner jackets and the meeting with Carl (not his real name), my Australian investor and finance partner, was warm and cordial. I knew he would be catching a train back to Westchester since he was just joining us for drinks. After tippling at the bar and Carl taking leave, I broached the subject of dinner. I hadn't known where to take the Basketball Star to dinner and had Carol make a number of reservations. It wasn't meant as a personality test, just as a few viable options he might enjoy, as he was in from out of town and I wanted him to be happy.

"I made a few reservations for dinner tonight," I offered, downing the last remnants of my martini.

"Any place is good with me," he said congenially.

"Since you're in from LA, we have choices: I thought we can go to the Upper East bistro [tony and sceney restaurant where millionaires and billionaires and their consorts hang], or sushi at [sceney and pricey West Side famed sushi restaurant where reservations are scarce], or if you're in the mood for a steak we can go to the [legendary and pricy Midtown steak house that caters to those who love a juicy strip and fried sides] or Miss Lily's, a cool Jamaican joint that just opened on the Lower East Side."

"Let's go to Miss Lily's," he said immediately, his eyes sparkling at the thought of spicy jerk and rice. "That's the one for me!"

"Perfect," I said, admiring his decisive choice and phoning the car and driver to take us downtown.

"Are you sure? It's all the way downtown," the Star offered graciously. "Is that OK for you?"

"Really, it's exactly where I want to go," I said.

Once settled into our back booth, my favorite table, the waitress read us a list of specials.

"We'll take the Ackee dip and plantains, the jerk wings, and the cod fritters. Don't forget the Blackwell rum with pineapple juice," I said as we surveyed the incredibly cool crowd, all taking in the authentic décor composed of a variety of album covers.

As the food started arriving, we strayed from business to warm personal conversation. One knows when fast friends are in the making. I can't say we wouldn't have bonded over sirloin and onion rings, or cod with miso, but as far as I was concerned, the Red Stripe and jerk wings said it was the start of a beautiful bromance.

I am on my way to the airport for an afternoon flight back to the city after the Wheels Up shoot. We are rounding hairpin turns. Driving on the other side of the road, British style, can be somewhat disconcerting for a New Yorker but I get used to it. We are making good time. We pass a sign reading 19 KILOMETERS TO RUNAWAY BAY.

Runaway Bay sounds like the perfect description of what a Jamaican parish should be: no problems, mon, no shoes, maybe some jerk on the Bar B, perhaps a bit of chutney, bamie, and maybe some rice and bean. Mikey, my Rasta driver, has the kindest smile and the most colorful UFO-shaped knit cap. As we round the curves, he munches on some fresh sugar cane. The landscape, stunning; beauty in contrast to the poverty. At least it's real, though, and has authenticity at every turn. As I look out the car window, I receive an e-mail from Chris who had journeyed to his thirty-five-hundred-acre farm, Pantrepant, in the center of Jamaica. (I call it the Jamaican Jurassic Park, with five-hundred-year-old banyan trees and gushing waterfalls.)

When I get back from Pantrepant, I am going to sell you a house at GoldenEye. It will be good for your writing, he wrote to my delight.

The idea of setting up my Microsoft Word where Fleming wrote all the Bond novels couldn't be a more magical or inspiring thought. A morning swim, Blue Mountain coffee, sand between my toes, and writing sounds like the ultimate fantasy. Add to that the fact that Dana loves it as much as I do and serves as my kayaking muse.

As the fall turns into winter, I think of the crowds soon to descend on places like Miami and St. Barths, where certain people I know are already making plans to send down their yachts well in advance (it's first come first serve for a slip) and will pay whatever it takes to be front and center with those who need to be front and center. Sounds like forced fun to me. Champagne toasts, caviar dreams, megayachts, and jerks who can't tolerate jerk spices; it couldn't sound less appealing. Jamaica is indeed a filter, and I think I'm going to have a house here.

And the best news of all is that Jerome and his wife won't want to come.

ACKNOWLEDGMENTS

To my beautiful and wonderful children, Talia, Lucas, and Georgia. Thank you for enriching my life on a daily basis. I love you to "infinitry."

Special thanks:

Thank you to Jared Kushner and my home at the *New York Observer*.

A true visionary, Faye Penn "discovered" me and molded and championed my column, and I am forever grateful.

To the *Observer*'s editor, Ken Kurson, I appreciate your keen eye and ardent support.

To Michael Gross, a greatly admired author, I am thrilled, honored, and grateful for your incredible foreword. Thank you!

To the legendary Liz Smith, thank you for your support and encouragement. I adore you.

To my dear friend Mort Zuckerman, thank you for your kind words and, most importantly, your friendship.

To my *Isn't That Rich?* team: my fabulous friend and editor Laura Yorke, and Carol Mann for your ongoing support. To the legendary Jane Friedman at Open Road, I am honored you are turning me into a "backlist author." Many thanks to Jack Turner and Jay Peterson at Matador for believing in my work. I am thrilled to partner with the powerhouse Meryl Poster, director extraordinaire; Azazel Jacobs; and my agent at CAA, Eric Wattenberg, on the upcoming TV show. An all-star team!

To the biggest supporters of *Isn't That Rich?*: Liz Anklow, Sean Cassidy, David and Jamie Mitchell, Jordan and Stephanie Schur, Jay and Amy Kos, Patty and Danny Stegman, Susan Kirshenbaum and Rob Perry, Muffie Potter Aston and Sherrell Aston, Chris Blackwell, Andrew Zaro and Lois Robbins, Marisa Acocella Marchetto and Silvano Marchetto, Baron Davis, Marc Glimcher, Ron and Stephanie Kramer, Harriet and Steven Croman, Stefani Greenfield and Mitchell Silverman, Glenn Pagan and Meg Blakey, Emanuele and Joanna Della Valle, Adriana Trigiani and Tim Stephenson, Kenny and Shoshana Dichter, Lisa and Richard Frisch, Judy Licht and Jerry Della Femina, Donny Deutsch, Bippy and Jackie Siegal, Stuart Elliot, Lisa Lockwood, Lorinda Ash, Oberon Sinclair, David Lauren and Lauren Bush Lauren, Steven and Ilene Sands, Rabbi Adam and Sharon Mintz, Mark E. Pollack, Morgan Spurlock, Lottie Oakley, Joyce and Michael Ostin, Jennifer Miller and Mark Ehret, Steve and Agatha Luczo, Richard and Lisa Plepler, Randy and Jan Slifka, Valerie Mnuchin and Bruce Moskowitz, Jill and Darius Bikoff, Leah Swarzman, Marc Schwartz and Suze Yalof Schwartz, Steven Swarzman, Julie and Billy Macklowe, Ali Cayne and Franklin Isaacson, Jon Landow and Joni Wilkins, Robert and Serena Perlman, Tim and Saffron Case, Harlan Peltz, Alison Brod, Jason and Ali Rosenfeld, Larry and Joan Altman, James Blank, Amy and John Kalikow, Daryl and Irwin Simon, Susie and Kevin Davis, Rona and Fred Davis, Alexis and Erik Ekstein, Vicky Benalloul, Richard Haines, Somers Farkas, Richard and Marcia Mishaan, Haley and Jason Binn, Charlie and Lauran Walk, Mark and Karen Hauser, Joe and Jessica Meli, Julie and Bruce Menin, Dustin Cohen, Liz Nickels, Susan Krakower, Chip and Susie Fisher, John Vassilaros and Alex Gersten-Vassilaros,

Amanda Ross, Bernard Peillon, Bill Gentner, Joseph Klinkov, Rob Wiesenthal, Richard Johnson, Ginia Bellafante, managing partner at NSG/SWAT Matt Garcia, and my long-time assistant, Carol O'Connell.

To my sources:

To Our Lady of the East River, I am only sorry I cannot reveal your identity, because no one would suspect you'd do it, but I am so very thankful.

To Southern Gentleman, I wish I could publish your name.

To one of the most famous seventies and eighties sitcom stars, Eileen Graybar (not real name), thank you, and may you get your comeback role.

And to all my sources who chose anonymity over speculation . . . I love and respect you, i.e., the Impossibly Blond and Glamorous Socialite, Best Man and Second Wife, the Social Powerhouse and Real Estate Mogul, the Silver Fox and L'actrice, Demoiselle, Brother from Another Mother, Blond Hollywood Wife, Hollywood Mogul, Fifth Avenue Heir, International Playboy Posse, Park Avenue Princess, British Socialite, Blond Millbrook Sportsman, Jonny Van der Klump, Queen of Couture, Principessa, Lily Whitebread, the Aging Platinum Benefactress, Cash and Charry, Resort Friend, and Hamptons Neighbor . . . to name a few. Life is richer with you all in it.

To the Open Road team: thank you to Tina Pohlman, David Adams, Nicole Passage, Mauricio Díaz, Andy Ross, Rachel Krupitsky, and Mary McAveney.

Thank you to my family. You know how much I love you.

And to all the people who gave me *attitude* and were *shady* about the column . . . all I can say is, you're going to miss a really great book party . . .

ABOUT THE AUTHOR

Richard Kirshenbaum is one of the most exciting personalities in New York City advertising. In 1987, at age twenty-six, he cofounded the Kirshenbaum Bond + Partners agency, which pioneered such innovative concepts as the pop-up store, sidewalk advertising, and other forms of high-visibility guerrilla marketing. At the time of its sale, KBP was the largest independent ad agency in the United States, with one billion dollars in billing. In 2011 Kirshenbaum launched NSG/SWAT, a high-profile boutique branding agency that works with entrepreneurs and emerging companies. He is also cofounder, with music icon Chris Blackwell, of Blackwell Fine Jamaican Rum.

Kirshenbaum has lectured at Harvard Business School, has appeared on *20/20*, was named to *Crain's New York Business*'s "40 under Forty" list, was inducted into the Advertising Hall of Fame in 2000, and snagged second place on a list of the top one hundred US entrepreneurs. He is the author of the business book *Under the Radar*; the relationship guide *Closing the Deal*, which has been translated into nine languages; the advertising memoir *Madboy*, an Amazon bestseller; and *Isn't That Rich?*, a compilation of essays from his *New York Observer* column. Kirshenbaum is an accomplished playwright, and his work has been produced by David Mamet's Atlantic Theater Company. He has also contributed to *Us Weekly*'s "Fashion Police" feature and has written comedy for the legendary Joan Rivers, among others.

EBOOKS BY
RICHARD KIRSHENBAUM

FROM OPEN ROAD MEDIA

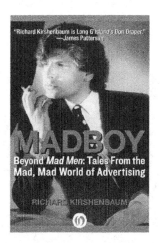

Available wherever ebooks are sold

OPEN ROAD
INTEGRATED MEDIA

Open Road Integrated Media is a digital publisher and multimedia content company. Open Road creates connections between authors and their audiences by marketing its ebooks through a new proprietary online platform, which uses premium video content and social media.